Six Easy Home-Improvement Projects

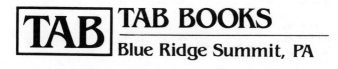

TAB BOOKS

Blue Ridge Summit, PA

FIRST EDITION
TENTH PRINTING

Printed in the United States of America

Library of Congress Cataloging in Publication Data

TAB BOOKS offers software for sale. For information and a catalog, please contact TAB Software Department, Blue Ridge Summit, PA 17294-0850.

Questions regarding the content of this book
should be addressed to:

   Reader Inquiry Branch
   TAB BOOKS
   Blue Ridge Summit, PA 17294-0214

Contents

Introduction

In this book, there are step-by-step instructions for do-it-yourself projects of interest to the beginning how-to enthusiast as well as the experienced jack-of-all-trades. Each of these practical, money-saving projects can be completed as described, or simply used as guidelines and starter ideas for more elaborate undertakings.

The projects in this book are only a sampling of the thousands of how-to projects available to members of the How-To Book Club. The chain link fence and the sun deck projects are from TAB Book 1508, *The Complete Book of Fences* by Dan Ramsey. The picnic furniture plans are from TAB Book 1454, *Constructing Outdoor Furniture, with 99 Projects* by Percy W. Blandford. The instructions for building barbecue pits and a brick patio and planter are from TAB Book 1204, *The Brickworker's Bible* by Charles R. Self. The skylight installation project is from TAB Book 1578, *Doors, Windows and Skylights* by Dan Ramsey.

Before you begin work, I suggest that you carefully read the instructions, select the site for the project, gather the appropriate tools, and keep this book handy. Good luck with your projects!

Steven Bolt
Senior How-To Editor

Project 1

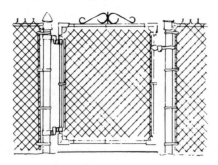

Chain Link Fences

Chain link is a most efficient fencing material for many homes. It offers maximum visibility, is adaptable to irregular ground, keeps out most intruders, allows clear air passage, and needs little maintenance to ensure a long life.

The biggest objection many people have to chain link fences is the lack of privacy. It's truly an "open fence." This objection can be overcome through landscaping; wood, metal, or plastic inserts; and with panels.

Chain link fencing is often less expensive to install and maintain than traditional wood fencing. You don't need a contractor to install it; you can do it yourself. Many fence supply companies will rent or loan you the special tools you need to install a chain link fence.

FENCE COMPONENTS

Installing a fence is easy. Here's a closer look at the basic components of a chain link fence.

Wire Size

Gauge designations can be and often are confusing for the consumer. Remember that the *smaller* the gauge number, the *bigger* (thus stronger) the wire.

Mesh Size

The size of the wire mesh (Table 1-1) is also important in determining the type of fence you ultimately have installed. These two items—wire and mesh size—affect price and durability.

1

Table 1-1. Standard Diamond Count for
Various Heights of Chain Link Fence—2-Inch Mesh.

Fabric Height	Diamond Count	
	11 Gauge	9 Gauge
36″	10½	10½
42″	12½	12½
48″	14½	13½
60″	17½	17½
72″	20½	20½
84″	24½	24½
96″	27½	27½
108″	31½	31½
120″	34½	34½
132″	37½	37½
144″	41½	41½

The size of the mesh is determined by measuring the distance between the parallel sides of the mesh. Common sizes are 2⅛ inches and 2 inches (mesh size for tennis court fencing is usually 1¾ inches in diameter). Larger mesh takes less steel and is not as costly.

Framework

The chain link fabric is supported by a framework consisting of line posts, terminal and corner posts, and top rail. They are held together by a set of specialized fence fittings (Fig. 1-1). This entire framework will be coated with either zinc or vinyl for long life and protection against the elements.

For residential fences, the line posts are normally 1⅝ inches O.D. (outside diameter). Wall thicknesses vary depending on your individual preferences for fence strength and rigidity. Terminal and corner posts might be 1⅞ or 2⅜ inches O.D.

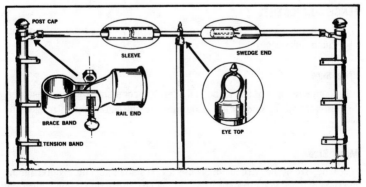

Fig. 1-1. Chain link fence posts, rails, and fittings (courtesy Builders Fence Co., Inc.).

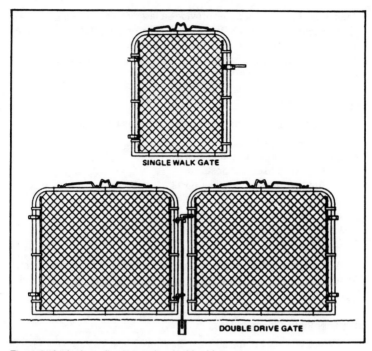

Fig. 1-2. A single-walk gate and a double-drive gate.

Top rail is normally 1⅜ inch O.D. It comes in 21-foot lengths joined by sleeves or swaged ends that slide together.

Gates

Gates should be of a sturdy construction with strong hinges, latches, and gateposts for long, trouble-free service (Figs. 1-2 and 1-3). Make

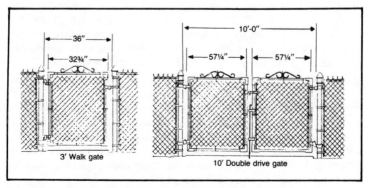

Fig. 1-3. Dimensions for single-walk and double-drive gates.

certain that the gate you order provides a large enough opening to easily accommodate items that you will be moving in or out of the enclosed area (such as garden equipment, lawn furniture, a recreation vehicle, etc.). You might want automatic closing and latching devices, these items and rolling gates are readily available.

INSTALLATION STEPS

There are eight simple steps to installing a chain link fence:

- ☐ Survey property lines.
- ☐ Locate and set terminal posts.
- ☐ Locate and set line posts.
- ☐ Apply fittings to terminal posts.
- ☐ Apply top rail.
- ☐ Hang fabric.
- ☐ Stretch fabric.
- ☐ Hang gates.

You need a posthole digger, a fence stretcher, a wire grip and stretch bar, cutting pliers, an adjustable end wrench, a tape measure, and a carpenter's level. See Figs. 1-4 and 1-5.

Step One: Survey Property Lines

Before you start to install your chain link fence, be sure your boundaries and property lines are legally established. Make sure that the location of your proposed fence lines does not exceed property lines. Place your fence line 2 to 4 inches *inside* your property line as insurance, and to avoid encroaching on adjoining property with the concrete foundations.

Step Two: Locate and Set Terminal Posts

Determine the location of end, corner, and gate posts (which are referred to as terminal posts). See Fig. 1-6. Distance between gateposts is determined by adding the actual width of the gate to an allowance for hinges and latches. Single walk gates require 3¾ inches for hinges and latches. Double drive gates require 5½ inches. A 3-foot walk gate should measure 32¼ inches wide. Adding 3¾ inches to the width means that the distance between posts (inside face to inside face) should be 36 inches.

Before digging postholes, determine if there are any underground cables or pipelines by contacting your local utilities. Figure 1-7 illustrates the right and wrong way to dig terminal and line postholes. Terminal postholes should be 10 inches wide at the top and 12 inches wide at the bottom. Line postholes should be 8 inches wide at the top and 10 inches at the bottom. If you're using a clamshell posthole digger, you can widen the bottom of the hole by simply angling the digger and scraping the sides, or you can use a small shovel to finish out the hole.

4

Using crayon or chalk, mark all posts for the correct height of fence you are installing (Fig. 1-8). Terminal posts should be set 2 inches higher than the fabric width. Line posts should be set 2 inches lower than the fabric width. Measurement C in Fig. 1-8 dictates the hole depth.

Set the terminal posts in concrete using a 1-2-4 concrete mix: 1 part cement, 2 parts sand, and 4 parts gravel (Fig. 1-9). Mix a fairly heavy solution because too much water weakens concrete and can result in cracked concrete. Use a carpenter's level to set posts plumb. Crown all post footings for water drainage by sloping concrete away from the post.

Because no two pieces of ground are alike or completely level, you must plan the contour of your installation in advance (Fig. 1-10). To make the top of your fence straight, you must compensate for ground level to a level line of sight. In some cases, it will be necessary to trench the ground at a particularly high ground level or, if the ground level is low, fill it with dirt. You can make a ground contour installation.

Step Three: Locate and Set Line Posts

Mark the grade line on all line posts by measuring from the top down (Fig. 1-11). Then measure the distance between terminal posts and check the line post spacing chart (Table 1-2) for the exact distance to allow between line posts.

Stretch a mason's line from outside to outside of terminal posts once you're sure the concrete has set up sufficiently. The line postholes should be lined up so that when they are set in the center of their holes ; their centers will line up with the terminal post centers. This means the outside faces of the line posts will be about ¼ inch inside of the line stretched

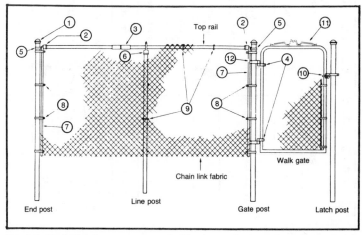

Fig. 1-4. Chain link fence components. Numbers refer to parts on the materials list in Fig. 1-5.

MATERIALS NEEDED FOR RESIDENTIAL CHAIN LINK FENCE

PIECES	ITEM—DESCRIPTION	QUANTITY TO USE	PRICE EACH
(1)	Fabric (50 feet per roll)	Divide total footage by 50 and round up	
(2)	Top Rail 21' x 1-3/8'' O.D. Swedged	Divide total footage by 21 and round up	
(3)	Line Post 1-5/8'' O.D.	Divide total footage by 10 and round up	
(4)	Loop Caps 1-5/8'' x 1-3/8''	Use 1 per Line Post	
(5)	Terminal Post 2-1/2'' O.D.	—	
(6)	Tension Bar	Use 1 per end or gate post, 2 per corner post	
(7)	Brace Band	Use 1 per Tension Bar	
(8)	Rail Ends 1-3/8''	Use 1 per Tension Bar	
(9)	Tension Band	Use 4 per tension bar or 1' per foot of fence height	
(10)	5/16'' x 1¼'' Carriage Bolts	Use 1 per tension or brace band	

(11)	Post Caps (Acorn Style) 2½"	Use 1 per terminal post
(12)	 Alum Cut Ties	Use 1 per foot of fence – Packaged 100 per bag
(13)	 Walk Gate (3' or 3½' wide)	—
(14)	 Double Drive Gate (10' or 12' wide)	—
(15)	 Male Hinge 2½"	Use 2 per walk gate and 4 per double drive gate
(16)	3/8 x 3 Carriage Bolts	Used with the male hinge, 1 per hinge
(17)	 Female Hinge 1-3/8"	Use 2 per walk gate and 4 per double drive gate
(18)	3/8 x 1-3/4 Carriage Bolts	Used with female hinge, 1 per hinge
(19)	 Fork Latch	Needed on walk gates only – 1 per gate

TOOLS YOU WILL FIND USEFUL IN INSTALLING YOUR FENCE

1. Post Hole Digger
2. Wheelbarrow, shovel and hoe to mix and transport concrete
3. Tape Measure
4. Level
5. String and Stakes or Mason's Line
6. Pliers
7. Fence Stretcher (Block and tackle, ratchet type power pull, etc.).
8. 1/2" x 9/16" Wrench or Crescent Wrench
9. Hacksaw or Pipe Cutter.

Fig. 1-5. Materials list for chain link fencing.

Table 1-2. Line Post Spacing.

Space	Set Post Apart	Space	Set Post Apart	Space	Set Post Apart	Space	Set Post Apart	Space	Set Post Apart
30 ft.	10 ft.	51 ft.	8 ft. 6 in.	71 ft.	8 ft. 9 in.	92 ft.	9 ft. 2 in.	112 ft.	9 ft. 4 in.
31 ft.	7 ft. 9 in.	52 ft.	8 ft. 8 in.	72 ft.	9 ft.	93 ft.	9 ft. 3 in.	113 ft.	9 ft. 5 in.
32 ft.	8 ft.	53 ft.	8 ft. 10 in.	73 ft.	9 ft. 2 in.	94 ft.	9 ft. 5 in.	114 ft.	9 ft. 6 in.
33 ft.	8 ft. 3 in.	54 ft.	9 ft.	74 ft.	9 ft. 3 in.	95 ft.	9 ft. 6 in.	115 ft.	9 ft. 7 in.
34 ft.	8 ft. 6 in.	55 ft.	9 ft. 2 in.	75 ft.	9 ft. 4 in.	96 ft.	9 ft. 7 in.	116 ft.	9 ft. 8 in.
35 ft.	8 ft. 9 in.	56 ft.	9 ft. 4 in.	76 ft.	9 ft. 6 in.	97 ft.	9 ft. 7 in.	117 ft.	9 ft. 9 in.
36 ft.	9 ft.	57 ft.	9 ft. 6 in.	77 ft.	9 ft. 7 in.	98 ft.	9 ft. 8 in.	118 ft.	9 ft. 10 in.
37 ft.	9 ft. 3 in.	58 ft.	9 ft. 8 in.	78 ft.	9 ft. 9 in.	99 ft.	9 ft. 9 in.	119 ft.	9 ft. 10 in.
38 ft.	9 ft. 6 in.	59 ft.	9 ft. 10 in.	79 ft.	9 ft. 10 in.	100 ft.	10 ft.	120 ft.	10 ft.
40 ft.	10 ft.	60 ft.	10 ft.	80 ft.	10 ft.	101 ft.	9 ft. 2 in.	121 ft.	9 ft. 3 in.
41 ft.	8 ft. 2 in.	61 ft.	8 ft. 8 in.	81 ft.	9 ft.	102 ft.	9 ft. 3 in.	122 ft.	9 ft. 4 in.
42 ft.	8 ft. 5 in.	62 ft.	8 ft. 10 in.	82 ft.	9 ft. 1 in.	103 ft.	9 ft. 4 in.	123 ft.	9 ft. 5 in.
43 ft.	8 ft. 6 in.	63 ft.	9 ft.	83 ft.	9 ft. 3 in.	104 ft.	9 ft. 5 in.	124 ft.	9 ft. 6 in.
44 ft.	8 ft. 9 in.	64 ft.	9 ft.	84 ft.	9 ft. 4 in.	105 ft.	9 ft. 6 in.	125 ft.	9 ft. 7 in.
45 ft.	9 ft.	65 ft.	9 ft. 3 in.	85 ft.	9 ft. 6 in.	106 ft.	9 ft. 7 in.	126 ft.	9 ft. 8 in.
46 ft.	9 ft. 2 in.	66 ft.	9 ft. 5 in.	86 ft.	9 ft. 7 in.	107 ft.	9 ft. 7 in.	127 ft.	9 ft. 9 in.
47 ft.	9 ft. 5 in.	67 ft.	9 ft. 7 in.	87 ft.	9 ft. 8 in.	108 ft.	9 ft. 8 in.	128 ft.	9 ft. 10 in.
48 ft.	9 ft. 7 in.	68 ft.	9 ft. 8 in.	88 ft.	9 ft. 9 in.	109 ft.	9 ft. 10 in.	129 ft.	9 ft. 10 in.
49 ft.	9 ft. 9 in.	69 ft.	9 ft. 10 in.	89 ft.	9 ft. 10 in.	110 ft.	10 ft.		
50 ft.	10 ft.	70 ft.	10 ft.	91 ft.	9 ft. 2 in.	111 ft.	9 ft. 3 in.		

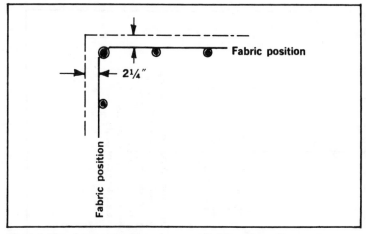

Fabric position

2¼"

Fabric position

Fig. 1-6. Planning post positions (courtesy Builders Fence Co., Inc.).

between the outside of the terminal posts. Dig the line postholes and set the line posts.

Stretch your mason's line taut 4 inches below terminal post tops and use it as a guide to align the height of line posts (Fig. 1-12). If it's necessary to adjust the height of any post either up or down, simply raise or lower the post (as illustrated) before the concrete sets up. Use your level to keep the post plumb while adjusting the height. It's best to let the concrete set up for about a day before continuing the installation of your chain link fence.

Step Four: Apply Fittings to Terminal Posts

After the posts are installed and the concrete has set, slip the tension and brace bands on to the terminal posts (Fig. 1-13). The tension bands should be spaced approximately 10 to 12 inches apart. Do not spread or distort the bands. All bolt heads for the bands should be on the outside of the fence, and the threaded ends should be on the inside. Apply all the terminal post caps.

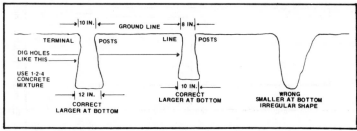

Fig. 1-7. The right and the wrong way to dig fence posts (courtesy Builders Fence Co., Inc.).

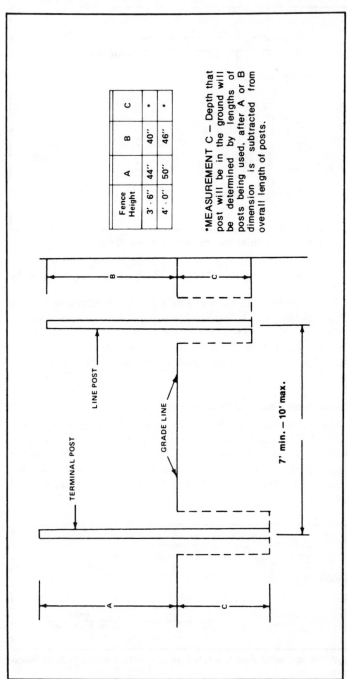

Fence Height	A	B	C
3' - 6"	44"	40"	*
4' - 0"	50"	46"	*

*MEASUREMENT C — Depth that post will be in the ground will be determined by lengths of posts being used, after A or B dimension is subtracted from overall length of posts.

TERMINAL POST

LINE POST

GRADE LINE

B

C

A

C

7' min. — 10' max.

Fig. 1-8. Estimating posthole depth (courtesy Builders Fence Co., Inc.).

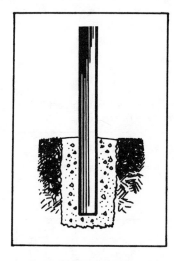

Fig. 1-9. Setting chain link fence posts (courtesy Builders Fence Co., Inc.).

Step Five: Apply Top Rail

The loop caps are now attached (Fig. 1-14). They are set with the top rail hole offset toward the outside of the fence (making flush the outside face of the top rail through the loop caps).

Join the top rail with swaged end where required (Fig. 1-14). The end of the top rail fits into the rail end fittings on the terminal post.

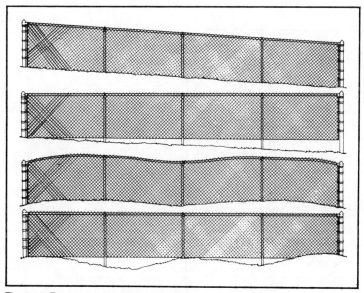

Fig. 1-10. Four ways of installing chain link fencing over uneven terrain (courtesy Builders Fence Co., Inc.).

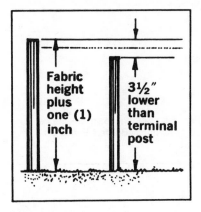

Fig. 1-11. Determining post height (courtesy Builders Fence Co., Inc.).

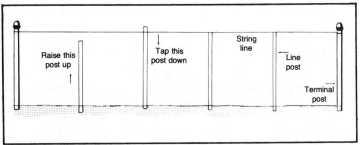

Fig. 1-12. Adjusting line posts to proper height.

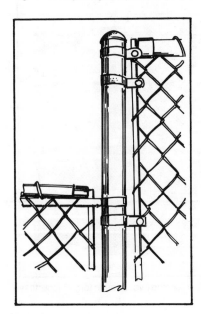

Fig. 1-13. Sometimes the top rail must be dropped.

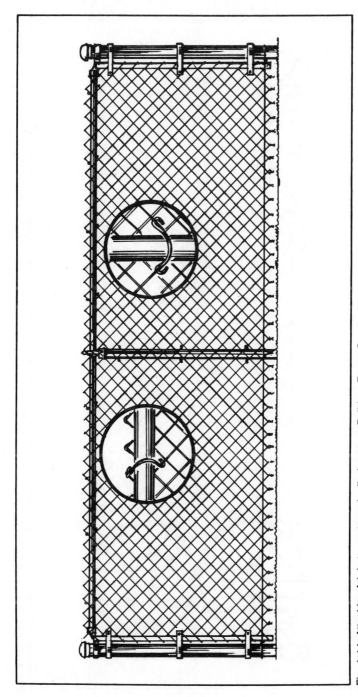

Fig. 1-14. Attaching fabric to posts and rails (courtesy Builders Fence Co., Inc.).

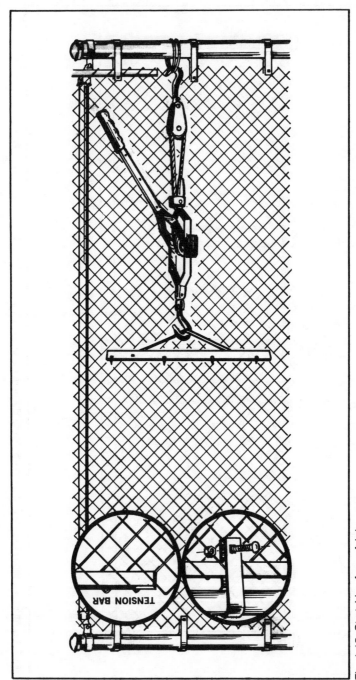

TENSION BAR

Fig. 1-15. Stretching fence fabric.

14

REMOVING FENCE FABRIC—to remove excess fence fabric. untie both top and bottom ends of wire at the spot you wish to terminate the section. Then twist this wire in corkscrew fashion until it comes completely out.

CONNECTING FENCE FABRIC—to join two sections of fence fabric, remove the end wire on **one** of the sections by untieing each end of the wire and twisting out in corkscrew fashion. Then pull the two sections together and connect with the single wire that was removed. Then retie each end. Note: Sometimes it is necessary to remove a second wire on the one end in order for the two sections to mesh.

Fig. 1-16. How to remove or connect fence fabric.

Step Six: Hang Fabric

After assembling the framework, unroll the fabric on the ground along the fence line starting at a terminal post. Slide the tension bar through the last link in your fabric. Attach this combination to the terminal post using the tension band and bolts provided (Fig. 1-15).

If more or less fabric is needed to span the opening, an additional amount can be connected or removed as shown in Fig. 1-16. The fabric should be on the outside face of all posts with either the knuckled or twisted edge at the top as preferred. It should be loosely attached to the top rail by a tie wire (Fig. 1-17).

Step Seven: Stretch Fabric

Fabric should be stretched from the terminal post already attached to the opposite terminal post. Insert the tension bar in the end of the fabric and

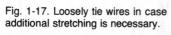
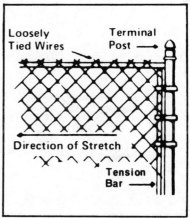

Fig. 1-17. Loosely tie wires in case additional stretching is necessary.

Loosely Tied Wires

Terminal Post →

Direction of Stretch

Tension Bar →

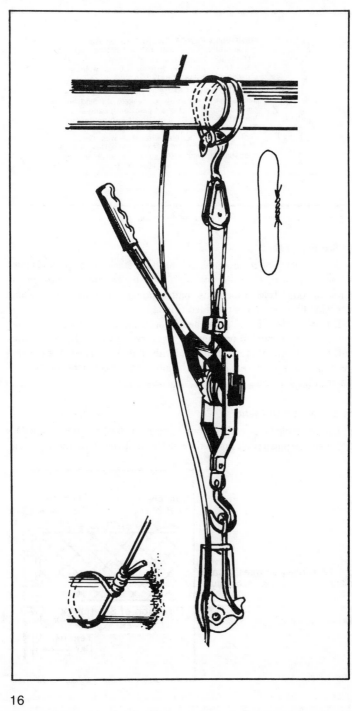

Fig. 1-18. Attaching the fabric stretcher (courtesy Builders Fence Co., Inc.).

16

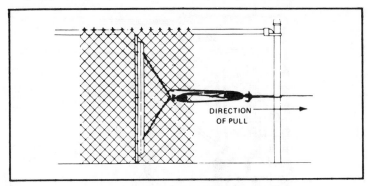

Fig. 1-19. Make sure the fabric is stretched evenly.

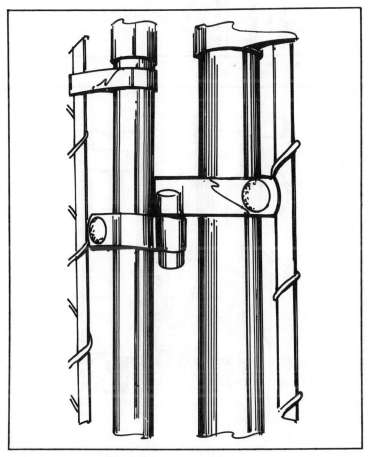

Fig. 1-20. Male and female hinge.

17

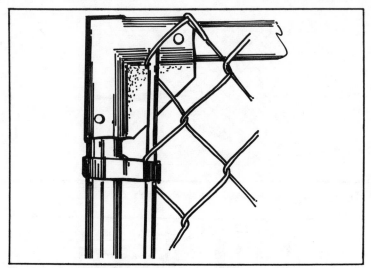

Fig. 1-21. Gate frame corner.

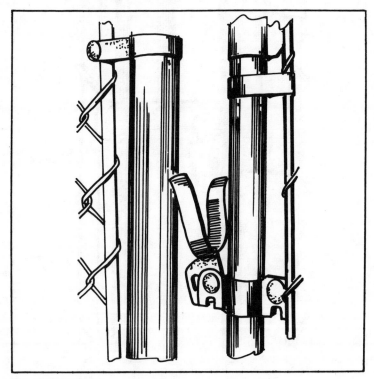

Fig. 1-22. Gate latch.

Fig. 1-23. Latch and chain for double-drive gates.

attach the fence stretcher to the bar (Fig. 1-18). A ratchet-type power pull, a large pair of carpenter's clamps, block and tackle, or a similar device can be used. Most wire stretching tools of this type can be rented or borrowed locally.

As you stretch the fabric test it for tension. It's stretched enough when it gives slightly. The top of the fabric should be located approximately ½ inch above the top rail to ensure proper height. After the fence fabric is sufficiently tight, remove the excess fabric, as shown in Fig. 1-19, and connect the tension bar to the post with tension bands. Fasten the fabric to the top rail and line posts with tie wires spaced approximately 18 inches apart.

For most residential installations, the fabric should be installed with the smooth edge up. If added security is necessary, you can install the fabric with barbs up.

Step Eight: Hang Gates

After the entire fence has been completed, apply male hinges to one of the gateposts. Hang the top hinge upside down to prevent the gate from being lifted off (Fig. 1-20). Loosely apply the female hinges on the gate frame and slip them onto the male hinges that have been installed on the gatepost (Fig. 1-21). Set the hinges to allow for full swing of the gate. Align the top of the gate with the top of the fence. Tighten all hinges securely. Install the gate latch for single gates (Fig. 1-22). Use the same procedure for double gates (Fig. 1-23) as on walk gates, but install a center latching device (fork latch).

Project 2

Sun Deck

Many outdoor structures are complementary to the fence and can easily be built by the do-it-yourselfer. These include decks, railings, benches, swings, walks, engawas, screens, pool enclosures, treillage, arbors, gazebos, pavilions, aeries, sun traps, tree houses, storage sheds, greenhouses, and other practical outdoor structures.

Few home improvements can match a wooden *deck* for usefulness, beauty, and enhanced value to a home. For adults, decks offer outdoor living space for entertaining, sunbathing, and dining. They provide an excellent outdoor play area for children. No advanced carpentry skills or sophisticated tools are needed. If you can hammer a nail, saw on a straight line, and read a level, building a deck should present you with no major problems. Figure 2-1 illustrates a popular 12- ×-12 sun deck, complete with construction details and materials list.

PLANNING

The location and design (Fig. 2-2) of your deck should be influenced by the following factors.

□ *Anticipated use:* private sunbathing, large parties, family recreation, outdoor cooking.

□ *Air currents:* allow the flow of gentle breezes and block out prevailing winds.

□ *Sunlight:* sun or shade.

□ *Privacy:* screen certain areas, avoid street noise, landscaping.

□ *View:* emphasize a good view or mask a poor one.

□ *Safety:* children, grandchildren, and senior citizens.

□ *Access to home:* adjoin kitchen, living room, or bedroom.

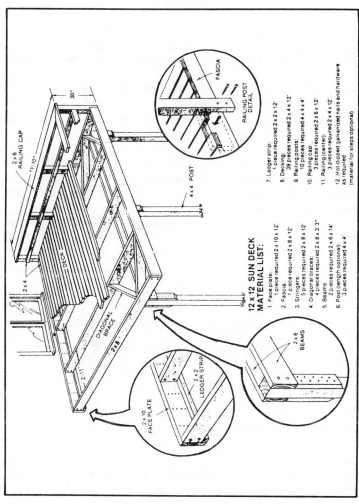

Fig. 2-1. Detailed plans for a 12-x-12-foot sun deck (courtesy Wolmanized pressure-treated lumber).

12 x 12 SUN DECK MATERIAL LIST:

1. Face plate:
   1 piece required 2 x 10 x 12'
2. Fascia:
   1 piece required 2 x 8 x 12'
3. Stringers:
   5 pieces required 2 x 8 x 12'
4. Diagonal braces:
   4 pieces required 2 x 8 x 3'3"
5. Beams:
   2 pieces required 2 x 6 x 14'
6. Post (length optional):
   3 pieces required 4 x 4'
7. Ledger strip:
   1 piece required 2 x 2 x 12'
8. Decking:
   39 pieces required 2 x 4 x 12'
9. Railing posts:
   10 pieces required 4 x 4 x 4'
10. Railing cap:
    3 pieces required 2 x 6 x 12'
11. Railing (center):
    3 pieces required 2 x 4 x 12'
12. Hot-dipped galvanized nails and hardware
    as required
    (material for steps optional)

21

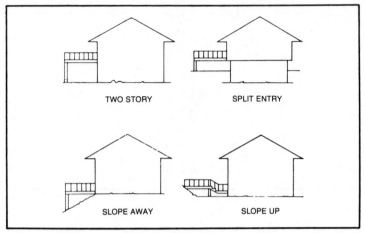

Fig. 2-2. Locating your deck (courtesy Wolmanized pressure-treated lumber).

☐ *Terrain:* elevated deck, ground level, split level.
☐ *Personal needs and preferences.*

Decks originally gained popularity as a way of adding outdoor living space on hillside lots. Many decks today are built on level ground where they offer firm, dry footing close to the home.

Decks can be built just inches high or elevated well above the ground (Fig. 2-3). They can be freestanding or attached to the home or other building. They can even be built as a second story above a garage, carport, or other roofed structure.

Make certain the deck does not seal access to any utility or drainage lines. Always be sure of the location or depth of buried electric, telephone, gas, water, or sewer lines. Ask your utility companies.

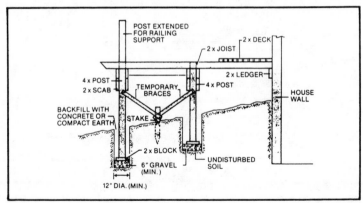

Fig. 2-3. Planning decks over a slope (courtesy Wolmanized pressure-treated lumber).

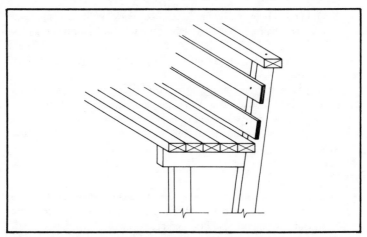

Fig. 2-4. Typical wooden bench construction (courtesy Western Wood Products Association).

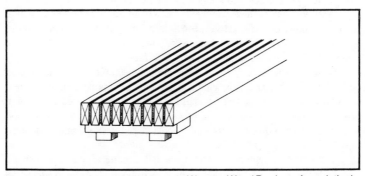

Fig. 2-5. Simple seating design (courtesy Western Wood Products Association).

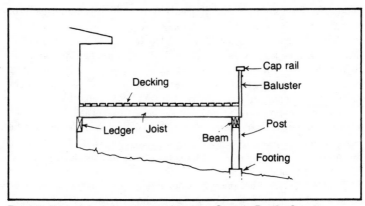

Fig. 2-6. Typical deck components (courtesy Georgia-Pacific Corp.).

23

Keep in mind how you intend to use your deck. Will it accommodate benches, lounge chairs, or perhaps a table for outdoor dining? See Figs. 2-4 and 2-5. How many people will be using the deck at any given time? These are elements that must be considered in planning for proper size and design.

Once you've decided on the basic size, shape, and location of your deck, check local building codes. You might find there are restrictions as to height and size within your subdivision or community. A construction permit will probably be needed, but don't apply for one until you've finalized your plans.

DESIGN

Decks consist of six parts: footings, posts, beams, joists, decking, and railings (Fig. 2-6). In planning for these you have three basic considerations: function, structural stability, and appearance.

The aesthetics of your deck will probably be most noticeable in your choice of railing and decking. The location of posts and beams can have a major effect on the appearance of a raised deck.

In almost every instance, your choice lies between several small pieces of lumber or comparatively fewer large ones. A railing might be held by 2-×-4 posts spaced every 16 inches or less, or it might have 4-×-4 posts capped by a 2-×-6 spaced as far apart as 8 feet.

Look at various deck plans. Inspect decks completed by friends and neighbors to help you decide what you like best. A popular choice is 2-inch thick lumber in widths of 4 or 6 inches (wider boards could present warping problems. These can be alternated to make more interesting patterns. You'll want to use pressure-treated wood and rustproof galvanized fasteners.

Tables 2-1 through 2-4 will help you in designing your own deck using lumber with 1200 psi (pounds per square inch) bending stress rating and a live load of 40 psf (pounds per square foot). The design and contruction information is for normal usage. If special load conditions are anticipated or unusual circumstances exist, consult a designer.

Let's say that your deck will extend 8 feet from the house and be 14 feet long. If it's to be just above ground level, there's little need for a railing. Higher decks call for a sturdy railing using 4-×-4 posts or something comparable. One of the best ways is to extend the posts supporting the deck so they also support the railing. But this isn't always possible.

Figure 2-7 shows that 4-×-4 posts can be up to 6 feet apart if capped by a 2×6. Rail height should be between 30 and 40 inches. Side rails can be made of nominal 2-inch lumber. The fastening system used will depend on the preferred rigidity; this is especially true when anchoring to stub cantilevered posts.

Table 2-1 shows the appropriate beam size. The distance between the house and the beam is 8 feet. A 4-×-8 beam allows a span of 7 feet between posts, that is a convenient figure for a deck 14 feet long. A beam can be a

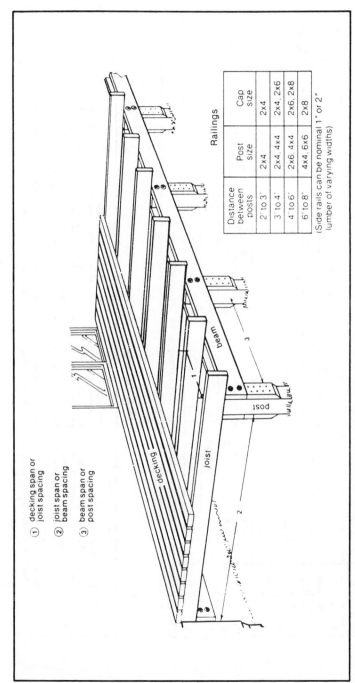

Railings

Distance between posts	Post size	Cap size
2' to 3'	2x4	2x4
3' to 4'	2x4, 4x4	2x4, 2x6
4' to 6'	2x6, 4x4	2x6, 2x8
6' to 8'	4x4, 6x6	2x8

(Side rails can be nominal 1" or 2" lumber of varying widths)

① decking span or joist spacing

② joist span or beam spacing

③ beam span or post spacing

Fig. 2-7. Planning a deck (courtesy Wolmanized pressure-treated lumber).

Table 2-1. Minimum Beam Sizes.

Length of Span (ft.)	Spacing between beams (ft.)						
	4	5	6	7	8	9	10
6	4 × 6	4 × 6	4 × 6	4 × 8	4 × 8	4 × 8	4 × 10
7	4 × 8	4 × 8	4 × 8	4 × 8	4 × 8	4 × 10	4 × 10
8	4 × 8	4 × 8	4 × 8	4 × 10	4 × 10	4 × 10	4 × 12
9	4 × 8	4 × 8	4 × 10	4 × 10	4 × 10	4 × 12	*
10	4 × 8	4 × 10	4 × 10	4 × 12	4 × 12	*	*
11	4 × 10	4 × 10	4 × 12	4 × 12	*	*	*
12	4 × 10	4 × 12	4 × 12	4 × 12	*	*	*

*Beams larger than 4 × 12 recommended. Consult a designer for appropriate sizes.

Table 2-2. Minimum Post Sizes.

Height (ft.)	Load area (sq. ft.) = beam spacing × post spacing				
	48	72	96	120	144
Up to 6	4 × 4	4 × 4	6 × 6	6 × 6	6 × 6
Up to 9	6 × 6	6 × 6	6 × 6	6 × 6	6 × 6

Vertical loads figured as concentric along post axis. No lateral loads considered.

26

Table 2-3. Maximum Allowable Spans for Spaced Deck Boards.

Maximum allowable span (inches)		
Laid flat		Laid on edge
2 x 4	2 x 6	2 x 4
32	48	96
Though able to support greater spans, the maximum spans will result in undesirable deflection or springiness in a deck.		

single piece of the dimension specified or built up from two smaller pieces (either nailed together or placed a few inches apart on either side of a post). Note, however, that two 2×8s are not equivalent to a 4×8 in *actual* dimensions.

To calculate the size post needed, multiply the beam spacing (8 feet) by the post spacing (7 feet). This gives you the load area: 56 feet. Table 2-2

Table 2-4. Maximum Allowable Spans for Deck Joists.

Joist size (inches)	Joist spacing (inches)		
	16	24	32
2x6	9'-9"	7'-11"	6'-2"
2x8	12'-10"	10'-6"	8'-1"
2x10	16'-5"	13'-4"	10'-4"

shows that a 4-×-4 post is adequate for a load area less than 72 square feet and a post height under 6 feet.

Decking in this example will be 2-×-6 boards laid flat. Table 2-3 shows the safe spans for the decking.

Refer to Table 2-4. As in our example, your joists must span the 8 feet between the house and the outer beam. That can be achieved with 2-×-8

Table 2-5. Lumber Scale of Board Feet per Timber.

Length of Timber	8	10	12	14	16	18	20	22	24
1 × 4	2⅔	3⅓	4	4⅔	5⅓	—	—	—	—
1 × 6	4	5	6	7	8	—	—	—	—
1 × 8	5⅓	6⅔	8	9⅓	0⅔	—	—	—	—
2 × 4	5⅓	6⅔	8	9⅓	10⅔	12	13⅓	—	—
2 × 6	8	10	12	14	16	18	20	—	—
2 × 8	10⅔	13⅓	16	18⅔	21⅓	24	26⅔	—	—
2 × 10	13⅓	16⅔	20	23⅓	26⅔	30	33⅓	—	—
2 × 12	16	20	24	28	32	36	40		
4 × 4	10⅔	13⅓	16	18⅔	21⅓	24	26⅔	—	—
4 × 6	16	20	24	28	32	36	40	—	—
6 × 6	24	30	36	42	48	54	60	66	72

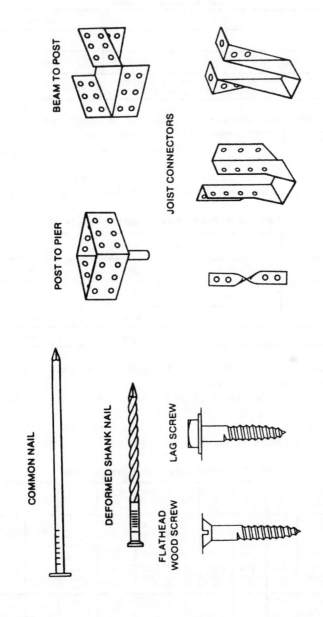

BEAM TO POST

POST TO PIER

JOIST CONNECTORS

COMMON NAIL

DEFORMED SHANK NAIL

FLATHEAD WOOD SCREW

LAG SCREW

28

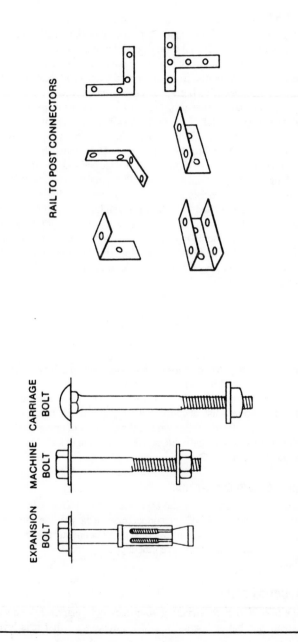

Fig. 2-8. Accessories and connectors used in constructing decks and fences (courtesy Wolmanized pressure-treated lumber).

29

joists spaced 32 inches apart. The 32-inch spacing is within the maximum span of 48 inches allowable for the 2-×-6 decking.

ESTIMATING

After deciding the type, space, and size of deck you'll build, the next step is to estimate the materials you'll need. If you use a ready-made design with a materials list, this work is already done for you. If you design your own deck or use a variation from a standard plan, you'll have to estimate material requirements. It's better to overestimate because you can always use excess material in other projects, such as benches or planter boxes.

Draw a simple sketch of the deck: decking, rails, footings, posts, and beams. The best scale is ¼ inch per foot. To save money, stick to standard lumber sizes and lengths to the fullest extent possible. Deck boards are usually stocked 2-×-4, 2-×-6, or 2-×-10 inch and 8-, 10-, 12-, 14-, and 16-foot lengths. Allow ¼-inch to ½-inch spacing between boards.

Prepare your materials list by dimensions and lengths for posts, beams, decking, stairs, and railings. Although lumber is sold at retail on a unit basis—so much for a 12-foot 2×4, etc.—you might also want to calculate your requirements in terms of total board feet. To determine the board footage in a piece of lumber, multiply the *thickness* in inches by the *width* in inches by the *length* in feet. Divide the total by 12. The formula is expressed as follows:

$$\frac{T \times W \times L}{12} = \text{Board feet}$$

The board-feet measure for various standard sizes and lengths of lumber can also be calculated by using Table 2-5.

After estimating your lumber requirements, review your design sketch and compile a list of the hardware you'll need: nails, bolts, joist hangers, and other fasteners, as well as the quantity of gravel and concrete needed. It's better to overestimate so you won't have to interrupt work for a trip for additional supplies.

ACCESSORIES AND CONNECTORS

Some special connectors and accessories that you should be familiar with are shown in Fig. 2-8. These connectors are easy to use and yet give a strong, long-lasting connection. Make sure all connectors, nails, screws, bolts, and related hardware are hot-dipped galvanized or otherwise rustproof.

CONSTRUCTION STEPS

The first step in constructing your deck is to mark off the deck area using string and batter boards (Fig. 2-9). Make sure that it is level and

Fig. 2-9. Remove grass under your deck before installation (courtesy Wolmanized pressure-treated lumber).

square. The string will help you visualize the size and appearance of the finished deck, and will also serve as a guide for excavating and post placement (Fig. 2-10).

To square the site with a string, first attach the string to the house and/or batter boards. Make sure it's level. Then use a felt tip marker to mark the string 3 feet from the corner in one direction and 4 feet from the corner in the other direction. When the diagonal connecting these two points is 5 feet, you have a right triangle. The angle at the corner will be 90 degrees.

The second step is to prepare the site. With a space or sod cutter, remove sod to a depth of 2 or 3 inches. Uncover an area about 2 feet larger than the planned deck. It's unlikely that grass will be able to grow in the shadow of your deck, so you might transfer the sod to a bare spot in your yard where it will be useful. To prevent weeds and unwanted vegetation

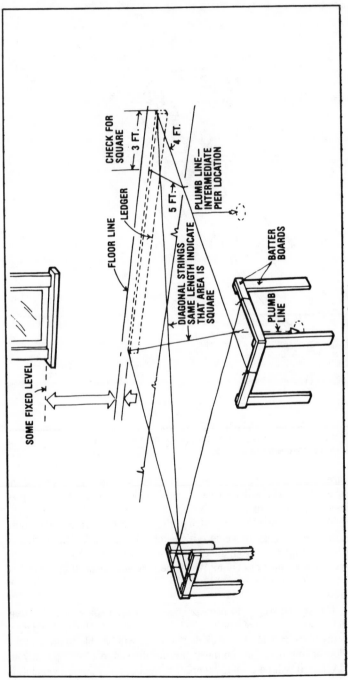

Fig. 2-10. How to measure and lay out your deck (courtesy Georgia-Pacific Corp.).

Fig. 2-11. Position and level upright posts (courtesy Wolmanized pressure-treated lumber).

from growing up through the deck, spread a sheet of polyethylene film over the area. You'll have to slit this to embed posts in the ground. After the posts have been installed, cover the sheet with gravel, pebbles, or bark chips.

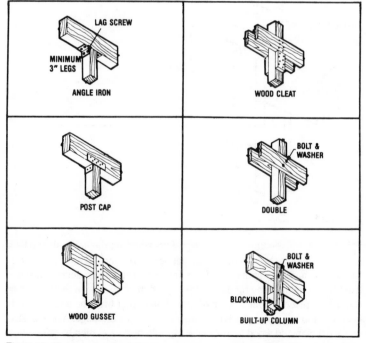

Fig. 2-12. Six ways to attach beams to posts (courtesy Georgia-Pacific Corp.).

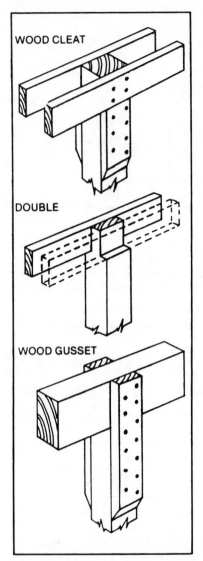

WOOD CLEAT

DOUBLE

WOOD GUSSET

Fig. 2-13. Methods for fastening beams and posts (courtesy Wolmanized pressure-treated lumber).

Locate and dig holes for footings. In normal soil the holes should be a minimum of 24 inches deep. The actual depth will depend on the height of the column and the depth of the frost line. Posts should go deeper than the frost line to avoid heaving during freeze and thaw cycles. In the bottom of the holes, place a 6-inch layer of gravel and tamp firm, or pour a 3-inch concrete footing and top it with gravel to allow for drainage. You can also use a Wolmanized wood footer plate. Upright posts can then be positioned on this base (Fig. 2-11).

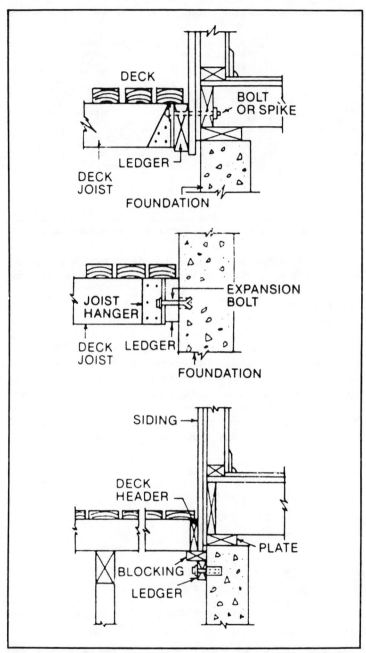

Fig. 2-14. Various ledgers and deck components (courtesy Wolmanized pressure-treated lumber).

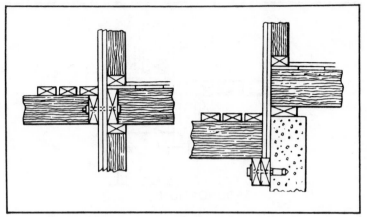

Fig. 2-15. Installing ledgers (courtesy California Redwood Association).

If concrete collars are used, taper the tops downward and away from the posts for drainage. When setting the posts, make sure they are plumb and in alignment with one another. Use a carpenter's level to check for vertical alignment.

The fourth step is to secure beams to the posts (Fig. 2-12). Using a string and level, find the desired deck heights on the posts. By subtracting the thickness of the deck board, joist, and beam (use the actual dimensions and not the nominal one), you'll have determined the correct spot for the bottom side of the beam. Cut the post at that point and fasten the beam on top by one of the methods shown in Fig. 2-13. If the posts are also serving as railing supports, they cannot be sawed off. Beams should be fastened to their sides. Double beams equaling a single beam of their combined thickness, can be installed instead of single beam supports.

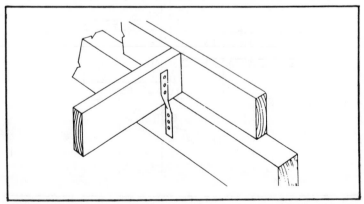

Fig. 2-16. Attaching the deck to the ledger (courtesy Wolmanized pressure-treated lumber).

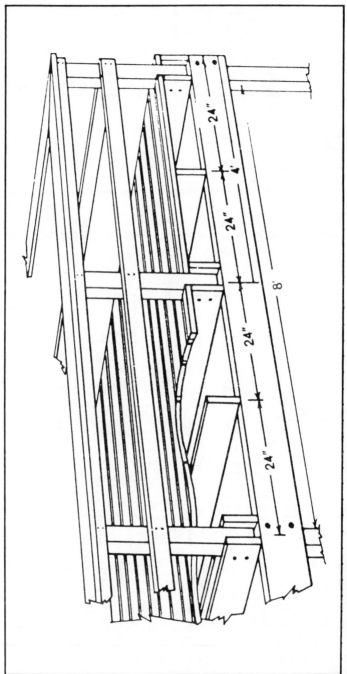

Fig. 2-17. Outside joists (courtesy Wolmanized pressure-treated lumber).

37

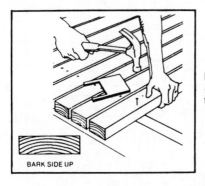

Fig. 2-18. Installing deck boards (courtesy Wolmanized pressure-treated lumber).

BARK SIDE UP

Step five involves attaching the joists to the house and beams (Fig. 2-14). Joists are attached to the house with joist hangers or supported by a ledger strip—a board secured to the house (Fig. 2-15). The placement of the ledger determines the level of the deck floor. Position it at the correct height and make sure it's horizontal (Fig. 2-16).

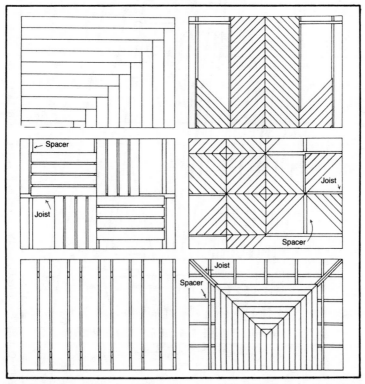

Fig. 2-19. Popular deck patterns (courtesy Wolmanized pressure-treated lumber).

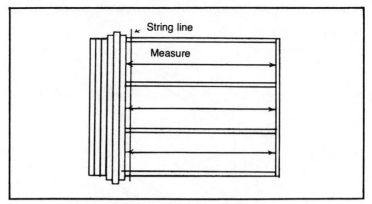

Fig. 2-20. Measure after installing every third or fourth board to make sure your deck will be square (courtesy Wolmanized pressure-treated lumber).

Fig. 2-21. Once boards are installed, you can lay a straightedge and trim the edge of your deck (courtesy Wolmanized pressure-treated lumber).

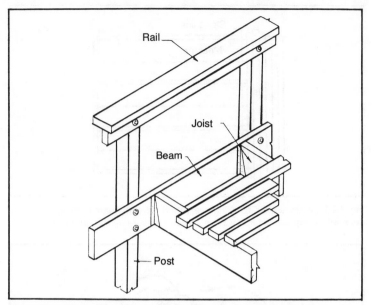

Fig. 2-22. Typical post railing (courtesy Wolmanized pressure-treated lumber).

When fastening to wood, ledgers can be held securely with lag screws. Drill a pilot hole first before driving the screws. If you have lap siding, a strip of the siding can be inverted and used as a shim to hold the ledger perpendicular. Expansion shields and lag bolts are needed for masonry construction.

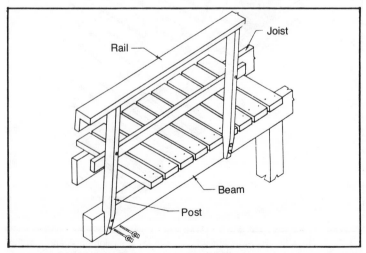

Fig. 2-23. Typical slant railing (courtesy Wolmanized pressure-treated lumber).

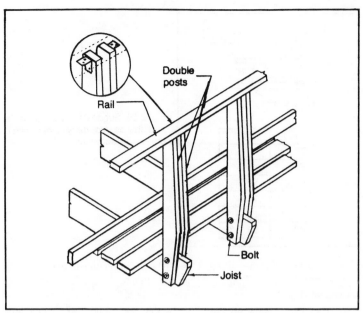

Fig. 2-24. Typical double-post railing (courtesy Wolmanized pressure-treated lumber).

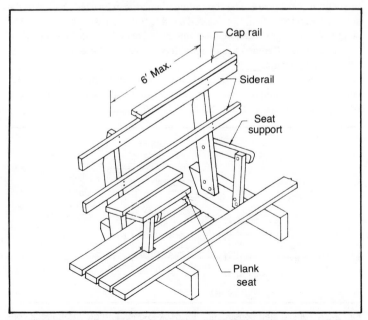

Fig. 2-25. Bench rail plans (courtesy Wolmanized pressure-treated lumber).

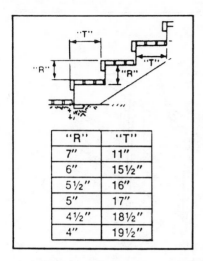

Fig. 2-26. Suggested ratios for risers and treads (courtesy Wolmanized pressure-treated lumber).

Install posts for the railing. This can be a continuation of the posts that support the deck, or railing posts can be bolted to the outside joist or joist extension (Fig. 2-17).

When using posts, they support the deck as in Fig. 2-17. Notice how the main posts continue up from the actual deck floor level and provide a sturdy railing post. Intermittent posts or spacer posts can be used between the main support posts. The top railing member can be easily nailed to the side of the main posts at the desired height. Posts can then be cut off. The height of spacer posts can be determined and added for additional support and appearance. Railing caps of suitable size can now be added along with additional side rails.

Step seven is to install deck boards using hot-dipped galvanized 12-penny nails. You might want to consider various nailheads and choose one with the appearance you like best.

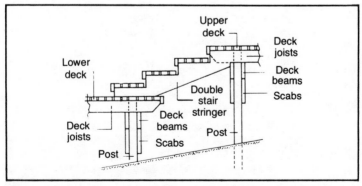

Fig. 2-27. Typical stair construction for deck-to-deck and ground-to-deck connections (courtesy Wolmanized pressure-treated lumber).

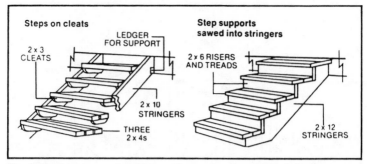

Fig. 2-28. Two types of stairway stringers (courtesy Wolmanized pressure-treated lumber).

Separate boards ¼ to ½ inch to allow for expansion and contraction. This can be quickly done using a spacer (Fig. 2-18) of the desired thickness.

Make your deck surface simple with boards of equal width set on joists or experiment by alternating plants of different widths, making parquet patterns, diagonal or herringbone designs, or using 2×4s set on edge (Fig. 2-19). Whichever pattern you choose, lay the deck board-side up. Make sure you measure as you go. If you discover that your spacing is off, adjust between the next three or four boards (Fig. 2-20). When you get near the end, start adjusting your space to avoid a gap at the end of your deck.

If you install decking using straight planking, you can trim your deck after nailing to assure a straight line (Fig. 2-21). Don't allow any overhang exceeding 1½ inches, or cut boards flush to the joist and add a fascia board.

The next step is to finish the railing. The safety and beauty of your deck are enhanced by its railings. They can be plain or very elaborate.

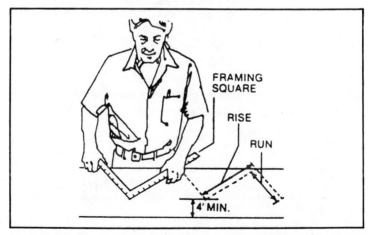

Fig. 2-29. Designing a stair stringer (courtesy Wolmanized pressure-treated lumber).

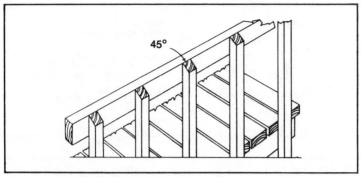

Fig. 2-30. Angle-cut rail post tops to improve moisture runoff (courtesy Wolmanized pressure treated lumber).

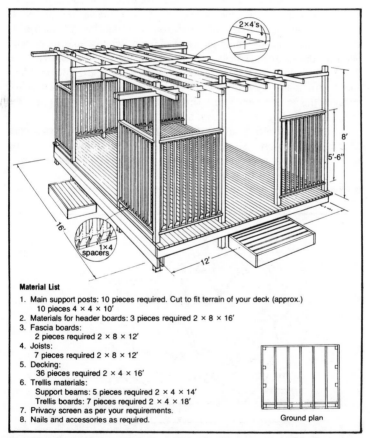

Material List

1. Main support posts: 10 pieces required. Cut to fit terrain of your deck (approx.)
   10 pieces 4 × 4 × 10′
2. Materials for header boards: 3 pieces required 2 × 8 × 16′
3. Fascia boards:
   2 pieces required 2 × 8 × 12′
4. Joists:
   7 pieces required 2 × 8 × 12′
5. Decking:
   36 pieces required 2 × 4 × 16′
6. Trellis materials:
   Support beams: 5 pieces required 2 × 4 × 14′
   Trellis boards: 7 pieces required 2 × 4 × 18′
7. Privacy screen as per your requirements.
8. Nails and accessories as required.

Ground plan

Fig. 2-31. Detailed plans for a 12-×-16-foot, trellis-covered privacy deck (courtesy Wolmanized pressure-treated lumber).

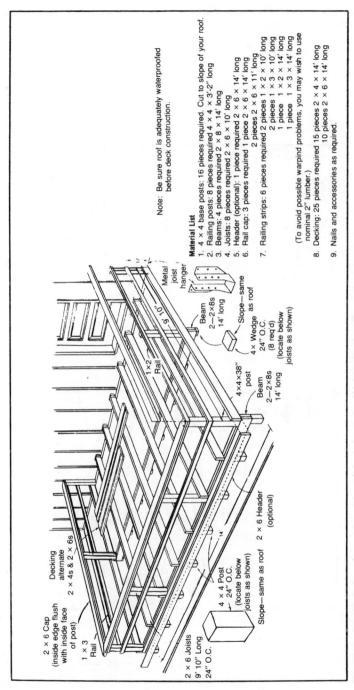

Note: Be sure roof is adequately waterproofed before deck construction.

Material List

1. 4 × 4 base posts: 16 pieces required. Cut to slope of your roof.
2. Railing posts: 8 pieces required 4 × 4 × 3'-2" long
3. Beams: 4 pieces required 2 × 8 × 14' long
4. Joists: 8 pieces required 2 × 6 × 10' long
5. Header (optional): 1 piece required 2 × 6 × 14' long
6. Rail cap: 3 pieces required 1 piece 2 × 6 × 14' long
   2 pieces 2 × 6 × 11' long
7. Railing strips: 6 pieces required 2 pieces 1 × 2 × 10' long
   2 pieces 1 × 3 × 10' long
   1 piece 1 × 2 × 14' long
   1 piece 1 × 3 × 14' long

(To avoid possible warping problems, you may wish to use nominal 2" lumber.)

8. Decking: 25 pieces required 15 pieces 2 × 4 × 14' long
   10 pieces 2 × 6 × 14' long
9. Nails and accessories as required.

Metal joist hanger

Beam
2—2×8s
14' long

Slope—same as roof

4 × Wedge
24" O.C.
(8 req'd)
(locate below joists as shown)

4×4×38"
post

Beam
2—2×8s
14' long

1 × 2
Rail

9' 10"

2 × 6 Cap
(inside edge flush with inside face of post)

1 × 3
Rail

Decking alternate
2 × 4s & 2 × 6s

2 × 6 Joists
9' 10" Long
24" O.C.

4 × 4 Post
24" O.C.
(locate below joists as shown)

Slope—same as roof

14'

2 × 6 Header
(optional)

Fig. 2-32. Detailed plans for a 10-×-14 roof deck (courtesy Wolmanized pressure-treated lumber).

45

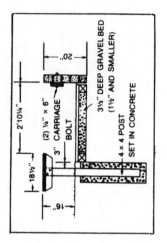

20"

2'10¼"

18½"

16"

3"

(2) ¼" × 6"
CARRIAGE
BOLT

3½" DEEP GRAVEL BED
(1½" AND SMALLER)

4 × 4 POST
SET IN CONCRETE

Material List

1. Deck
   8 pieces required 4 × 4 × 10'
   27 pieces required 2 = 4 × 10'
2. Benches: (6'-8" long & 8'-8" long)
   5 pieces required 4 × 4 × 4'
   5 pieces required 2 = 4 × 7'
   5 pieces requires 2 = 4 × 12"
3. Firepit
   40 pieces required 4 × 4 × 16"
   1 bag mortar
   2 pieces required 2 × 6 × 6'
4. Nails and accessories as required

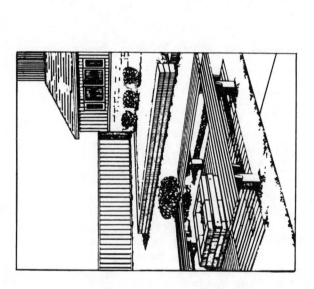

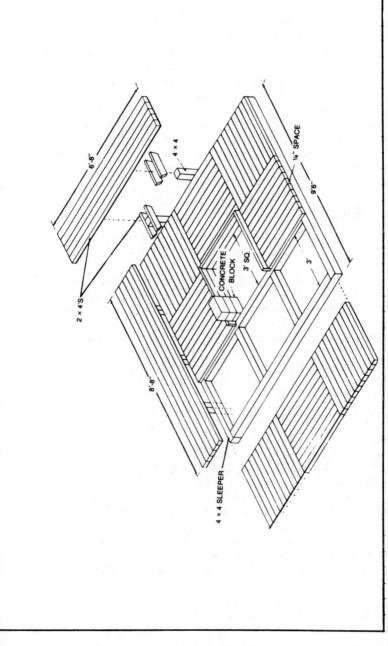

Fig. 2-33. Detailed plans for a 10-×-10-foot, fire-pit deck (courtesy Wolmanized pressure-treated lumber).

6'-8"

4 × 4

¼" SPACE

9'6"

2 × 4'S

CONCRETE
BLOCK

3' SQ.

3'

8'-8"

4 × 4 SLEEPER

Benches can be integrated into the railing on one or all sides (Figs. 2-22 through 2-25). Bench seats should be at least 15 inches wide and 15 to 18 inches above the deck floor.

Privacy screens can enhance the beauty of your deck and offer privacy. They can also be used effectively under an elevated deck to create a storage facility or hide an unsightly hillside.

The final step is to install steps. Measure the vertical rise and decide on the best riser size for each step. This will determine the number of steps needed. Figure 2-26 shows some recommended ratios of tread length to find the overall run of the stairs. See Fig. 2-27.

Figure 2-28 illustrates two types of stairway stringers; open, in which the treads are placed on sawed cuts; or closed, where concealed cleats support each tread. See Fig. 2-29.

You can purchase precut steps at many lumberyards. A call ahead might eliminate some of the more difficult angle cutting you would otherwise have to do.

ADDITIONAL CONSTRUCTION TIPS

☐ Always nail a thinner member to a thicker member.

☐ Drive nails at a slight angle toward each other for greater holding power.

☐ When toenailing, stagger opposing nails so they pass each other.

☐ Use annular- or spiral-shank nails for maximum holding power.

☐ To reduce splitting, drill a pilot hole about three-quarters of the nail's diameter. For dense or brittle wood, grind sharpness from nails or blunt the points by striking them carefully with a hammer. Blunt nails cut through; sharp ones pry apart.

☐ Place nails no closer to the edge than about half the board thickness, and no closer to the end than the board's thickness. When nailing closer to an edge, use drilled starter holes.

☐ Use 12d nails on nominal 2-inch decking. Use two at each joist with 2×4s laid flat; use three for 2×6s laid flat; and use just one for nominal 2-inch lumber on edge.

☐ Use a flat washer under the head with lag screws.

☐ Use washers under the nut and head of machine bolts and just under the nut of carriage bolts.

☐ When sanding or sawing treated or untreated wood, avoid inhaling dust. The fine dust particles are air pollutants and could cause nose and throat irritation. Avoid getting dust or wood chips in your eye. Eyes are extremely sensitive, and any type of foreign matter can cause irritation. Pounding nails should be done cautiously; small flying particles of metal can cause serious eye damage. Ask your dealer about dust masks and eye protection devices.

☐ Wear gloves to help avoid splinters.

☐ Maintain a clean shop. Don't leave sawdust or scrap lumber lying around because they pose fire and accident hazards. Pressure-treated wood should not be burned either indoors or outdoors. Any scrap should be disposed of in a government-approved landfill.

☐ Tops of upright structurals and joist ends should be beveled to a 30 to 45-degree angle for drainage to minimize moisture absorption (Fig. 2-30). Figures 2-31 through 2-33 show more plans for decks.

Project 3

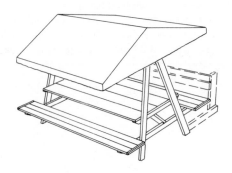

Picnic Table With Canopy

The common picnic table is a utilitarian piece of outdoor furniture, but it is more of a bench that does its job than a piece of decorative or personalized furniture for your yard or garden. It serves a valuable purpose in many public places. If you want something different on your own property, one way of enhancing its appearance and usefulness is to build it with a canopy, and possibly with backs to the seats. See Table 3-1.

This combination table/seats/canopy is first described without backs to the seats (Fig. 3-1), but seat backs are described later. Sizes suit an overall length of 96 inches, but the ends can be used with tables and seats of other lengths. The wood sections are intended for softwood and could be reduced slightly for hardwood.

The sizes (Fig. 3-2) allow for eating at a convenient height. The canopy gives ample clearance as you stoop to sit. The canopy overhang is not much, but there has to be a limit. Its width could be increased if you prefer.

If possible, set out an end, or half of it, full size on the floor to get the angles and sizes of the legs. Otherwise, it is possible to lay down a pair of legs and move them into the correct relative positions and mark angles and the positions of other parts on them. The ridge goes between the tops of the legs so that they are notched to suit, but cut them back enough to clear the slope of the canvas canopy (See A of Fig. 3-2 and A of Fig. 3-3). Join the legs under the ridge with gussets both sides (B of Fig. 3-3). The table rail (C of Fig. 3-3) and the seat rail (D of Fig. 3-3) have their ends beveled underneath and they go across the legs symmetrically and parallel with the floor. Measure carefully. Errors might not be obvious until assembly is complete. Then it will be too late for correction.

For strength, it will be best to bolt through these joints ; two ⅜ inch

Table 3-1. Materials List for Picnic Table with Canopy.

4 legs	4	×	84	× 2
2 seat rails	3	×	68	× 2
2 table rails	3	×	38	× 2
2 canopy rails	3	×	80	× 2
4 gussets	6	×	10	× 1
8 canopy rafters	2	×	98	× 2
1 ridge	4	×	102	× 2
2 canopy rails	2	×	98	× 2
4 table tops	9	×	96	× 2
1 table rail	4	×	38	× 2
2 table struts	3	×	54	× 2
6 seat tops	4	×	102	× 2
8 seat cleats	2	×	13	× 2
1 ridge	4	×	102	× 2
4 seat ends	4	×	13	× 1
with seat backs:				
Increase seat rails to	3	×	88	× 2
4 back supports	3	×	34	× 2
4 bottom rails	3	×	28	× 2
4 back rails	4	×	102	× 2

bolts at each position are suitable (A of Fig. 3-4). If you prefer to use screws, it is advisable to cut shallow notches for the rails in the legs to resist any tendency for the rails to slide down (B of Fig. 3-4). You could bolt through the gussets at the top, but screws should be strong enough there.

The seat and table rails are on the inside of the legs, but the canopy rail goes on the outside. That should also be bolted to the legs. Make sure it is parallel with the other rails (E of Fig. 3-3). A pair of rafters go from the ridge to its ends. They do not have to provide much strength. They can be nailed in place. Cut them to fit against the ridge (F of Fig. 3-3). At the other

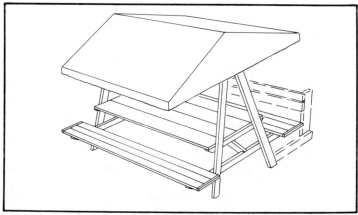

Fig. 3-1. A picnic table with a canopy.

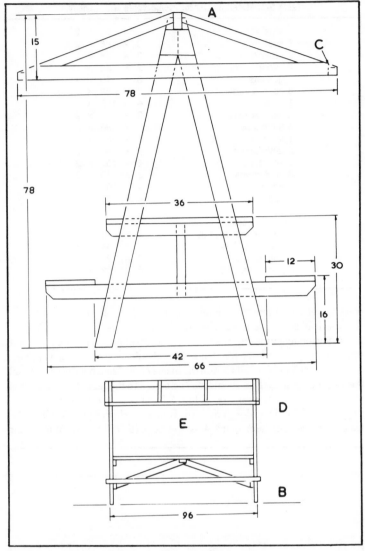

Fig. 3-2. Suggested sizes for a picnic table with canopy.

end, bevel them and the ends of the rail, down to 2 inches deep (G of Fig. 3-3), so that there is a smooth slope on the roof angle.

The table and its struts brace the whole assembly. It is recommended that four pieces, 9 inches wide, make up the top. Other widths available could be used. They need not all be the same. Allowing for planing to width, there will be gaps of ¼ inch or so between boards. Nail the top boards to their rails on the ends. Under their centers put a rail across. It can be cut a little short and its lower edge beveled so that it is inconspicuous and does not interfere with users.

The two struts go from the seat rails to the rail (B of Fig. 3-2 and C of Fig. 3-4). Notch them over the seat rails and cut the center notches so that each strut goes across the full width of the rail and its full depth is against the top boards (D of Fig. 3-4). Let the struts overlap each other on this rail so that they can be nailed to the rail and to each other. While doing this, check that the table and legs are square to each other. Measure diagonals from top and bottom corners of opposite legs. It will help to have the ridge piece in position, but not finally nailed until you are satisfied that the parts

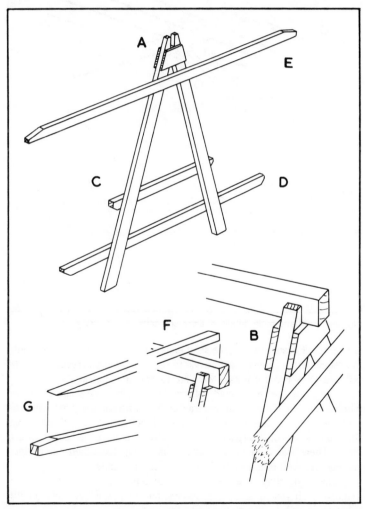

Fig. 3-3. Construction of the end frames of a picnic table with canopy.

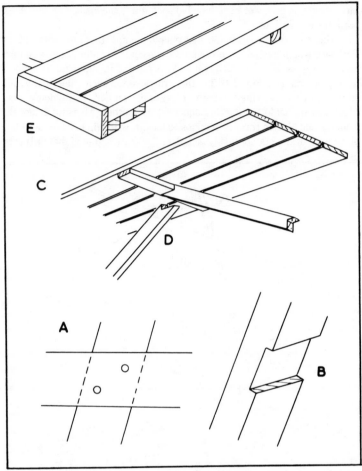

Fig. 3-4. Seat and table details of the picnic table with canopy.

are square. Because getting the strut ends correct is important, it will help to first cut a thin piece of scrap wood to size. Allow for corrections to it (if necessary) as you use it as a template for the actual struts.

The seats are shown made of three pieces, but you could use other widths. Like the tabletop, they are assembled with narrow gaps. The ends could be open, but they look neater closed (E of Fig. 3-4). Put cleats across the ends and two others spaced evenly between to brace the boards to each other. Then close the ends with strips that should have their outer edges and corners well rounded. Nail the seats to their rails.

Check the rigidity of the assembly at this stage. It should not flex lengthwise. If you consider it necessary, put metal brackets between the ridge piece and the inner gussets to the legs.

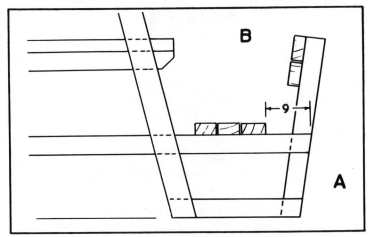

Fig. 3-5. Modifying the framework to provide a back to each seat.

To give shape and support to the canvas canopy, put lengthwise rails between the end rails (C and D of Fig. 3-2). Join them to the ridge with intermediate rafters (E of Fig. 3-2) to keep the shape and prevent the canvas from sagging. Sight along from the ends as you fit these rafters to check that you are keeping the slopes the same.

You could get a canvas cover made from paper templates, but light canvas can be sewn on a domestic sewing machine. That gives you an opportunity to get an exact fit. Assemble the panels inside out over the framework and pin them together on the lines that have to be sewn. Allow for the edges hanging down about 6 inches. Those edges could be turned under in a straight line or made scalloped. While sewing the seams, include pieces of tape at intervals long enough to tie round the framework at about 24-inch spacing.

Comfort is increased if the seats are given backs (Fig. 3-5). Construction is the same, as already described, except the seat rails should be made about 20 inches longer. The back angle will be about 10 degrees from vertical, or a little more, but make sure all four supports are the same. During the assembly of the ends, put the short bottom rails across the insides of the legs, and arrange the supports inside them and the seat rails (A of Fig. 3-5). If you want to fasten the table to the ground, it would be better to take these bottom pieces across in single lengths. Then brackets or pegs to the ground can be attached to them.

The backs are shown at the same height as the table, but they could be a few inches higher or lower if you prefer. Two rails similar to those of the seat are shown in B of Fig. 3-5. They should be stiff enough without intermediate supports. You could brace them to each other by putting short packings between them at one or two places. If the seat needs stiffening, you can add struts similar to those under the table. Place them from the bottom rails to other rails put across under the seat.

Project 4

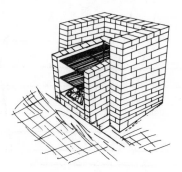

Barbecue Pits

This section contains instructions for building two projects: a mortarless barbecue and a mortared barbecue. Each project has a tool list, a material list, and directions for building the unit.

MORTARLESS BARBECUE

Because this barbecue is constructed without mortar, it is essential that the building site be absolutely level. A concrete slab provides the ideal surface. Be sure to obtain the grill racks before you actually begin construction. It is much easier to plan a barbecue around a grill than it is to buy a grill that will fit once the project is "complete."

Study Figs. 4-1 and 4-2 before you begin. Using a hammer and a 2 × 4, carefully tap in the bricks that support the grill racks. Hold the 2 × 4 edgewise against the bricks as you tap them.

Tools

    2-foot hand level
    Hammer
    2 × 4

Material

    236 solid bricks, 3¾″ × 2¼ × 8″
    Two grill racks

MORTARED BARBECUE

Choose the location for the barbecue with the prevailing winds in

Fig. 4-1. A mortarless barbecue is easy to build.

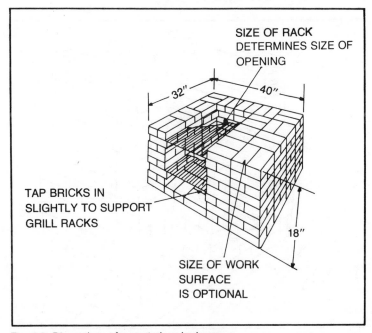

SIZE OF RACK DETERMINES SIZE OF OPENING

32"

40"

TAP BRICKS IN SLIGHTLY TO SUPPORT GRILL RACKS

18"

SIZE OF WORK SURFACE IS OPTIONAL

Fig. 4-2. Dimensions of a mortarless barbecue.

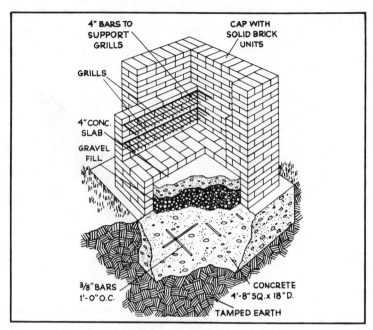

Fig. 4-3. Dimensions of a mortared barbecue.

Fig. 4-4. A mortared barbecue.

58

mind. Study Figs. 4-3 and 4-4 before you begin work. Excavate the site and pour the concrete. Be sure to place the reinforcing bars as shown in Fig. 4-5. Position the bars in a grid pattern and support them with bricks so that the grid is approximately in the center of the concrete. The bars can be wired together to form a unit.

Outline the barbecue on the concrete slab. Lay a few courses of brick without mortar to determine if the pattern works. Remember to allow for ½-inch mortar joints.

Begin by first laying the corner. The bottom bricks are bonded with mortar to the concrete slab. Build three or four courses at the corners and then fill in the walls. Use a hand level to frequently check the walls for plumb. As you build to the height of the grills, insert 4-inch sections of reinforcing bars for grill supports (Figs. 4-3, 4-4 and 4-6).

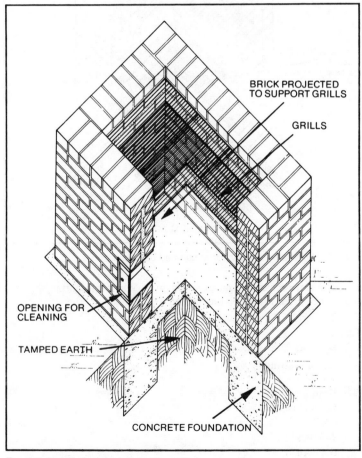

Fig. 4-5. Details for a small cooking grill.

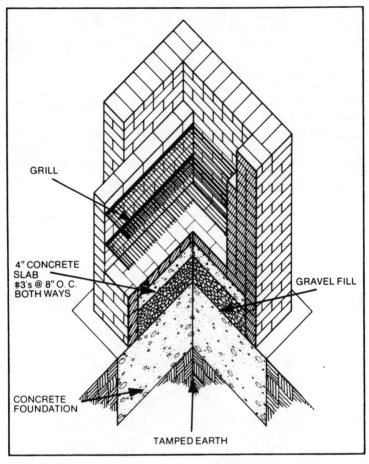

GRILL

4" CONCRETE
SLAB
#3's @ 8" O.C.
BOTH WAYS

GRAVEL FILL

CONCRETE
FOUNDATION

TAMPED EARTH

Fig. 4-6. Construction details for a mortared barbecue.

Use a trowel to clip off excess mortar. When the mortar becomes thumbprint hard, use a pointing tool to work the joints.

Tools

Hammer
Mason's string
Trowel
Hand level
Brick chisel
Chalk
Wooden float
Handbrush

Material

450 cored bricks, 3¾″ × 2¼″ × 8″

75 solid bricks, 3¾″ × 2¼″ × 8″

6 cubic feet of mortar

27 cubic feet of concrete for the foundation

1⅔ cubic feet of concrete for the hearthslab

20 reinforcing bars, ⅜ of an inch in diameter and of the following lengths:

      5 bars, 18″ long

      3 bars, 32″ long

      12 bars, 4″ long

Project 5

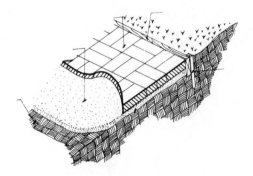

A Brick Patio and Planter

There are some general methods you should keep in mind before you begin to build the brick patio and planter described in this chapter. If you are using mortarless brick paving, remember that it has a tendency to spread at the edges if some sort of frame is not placed around the perimeter of the patio. This frame can be made of 2-inch wood (Fig. 5-1) or of a course of brick set in concrete or mortar (Fig. 5-2). If the edging is positioned prior to laying the brick surface, the edging can serve as a guide for drainage slopes.

Without proper drainage, brick paving can be subjected to excessive moisture that might result in the growth of fungi or molds, and the disintegration caused by repeated freezing and thawing. To counter such potential problems be sure to slightly slope the patio to one side or from the center of a rate of ⅛ to ¼ of an inch per foot. Slope the paving away from buildings, walls, or areas that will retain the flow of water.

Another potential problem can result from the upward capillary travel of moisture from soil that is heavily laden with soluble salts. Such salts can cause a powdery substance or strains to form on the brick paving. If the soil in your area contains soluble salts, install a "capillary break" of gravel (Fig. 5-3) to prevent the upward flow of moisture. This layer of gravel can be graded to obtain the power slope and placement of the bricks. A layer of sand can be substituted for gravel if soluble salts are not present in the base soil. Do not place a layer of sand over a layer of gravel; the sand will eventually sift into the gravel and cause uneven settlement of the brick paving.

A patio with a concrete slab base and mortared joint paving is the best way to counter the problem of ground swell caused by freeze/thaw cycles. If ground swell is not a problem in your area, a patio with mortared joints can easily be constructed without a concrete slab.

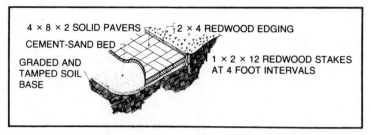

Fig. 5-1. The patio is framed with 2-inch redwood.

4 × 8 × 2 SOLID PAVERS   2 × 4 REDWOOD EDGING

CEMENT-SAND BED

GRADED AND TAMPED SOIL BASE

1 × 2 × 12 REDWOOD STAKES AT 4 FOOT INTERVALS

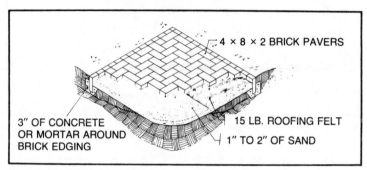

Fig. 5-2. Mortarless brick paving on a cushion of sand.

4 × 8 × 2 BRICK PAVERS

3" OF CONCRETE OR MORTAR AROUND BRICK EDGING

15 LB. ROOFING FELT

1" TO 2" OF SAND

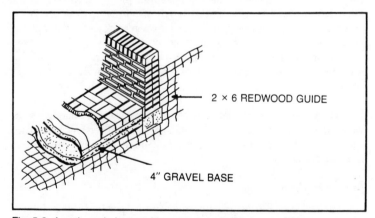

Fig. 5-3. A patio and planter with a cutaway showing a gravel base.

2 × 6 REDWOOD GUIDE

4" GRAVEL BASE

First, grade and tamp the subsoil to eliminate soft spots. Carefully screed a 1- to 2-inch cushion of sand over the subsoil. Lay the bricks in place with ½ inch of mortar between each unit (when using 3¾-×-8-×-2¼-inch bricks). Be sure to sweep the paving free of dry mortar because portland cement will stain brick if it is allowed to remain on the surface. Keep the paving damp for two or three days.

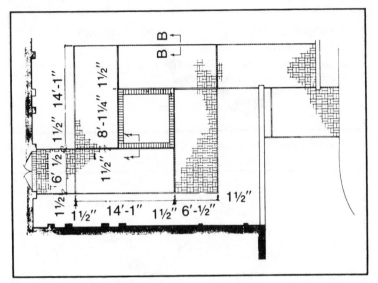

Fig. 5-4. A patio and planter layout.

To construct a patio without mortar joints, using 4-×-8-inch pavers, screed and tamp a 1-inch to 2-inch bed of sand over the subsoil. Next, roll out sections of 15-pound roofing felt, and place the felt sections over the sand. Lay the bricks on the felt. The felt stabilizes the base and helps prevent the growth of weeds and grass between brick joints. After all the bricks have been layed, sweep dry sand into the joints.

The patio layout shown in Fig. 5-4 is designed to be built in four sections to form a continuous surface around a large brick planter. Each section is approximately 6 × 14 feet, and the completed patio is slightly over 20 square feet.

The project can be completed over a few weekends or during a short vacation if the bricks are laid on a cushion of sand and cement. In climates where freeze/thaw cycles are common, the patio should be constructed on a concrete foundation.

LAYOUT AND EXCAVATION

Use stakes and string to outline the patio and planter. At the center of the line between stakes, suspend a line level. Remember to allow for a slope of ⅛ to ¼ inch per foot. The stakes should be marked in the direction the surface will drain. The marks are also used as excavation guides and later they can be used as a guide for laying the bricks.

The outside dimensions for the patio are 6 feet 3½ inches × 14 feet 4 inches. Allow 1½ inches for redwood framing and an additional ½ inch to 1 inch for fit. The planter is 8 feet 1¼ inches square. See Fig. 5-4.

Excavate 3½ inches deep for the patio section. For the planter, excavate a trench 3½ inches deep and 11 inches wide (form allowance) around the perimeter. Do not excavate the area within the planter.

During excavation, take measurements and frequently check the marks on the stakes. Stretch a line across the excavation and measure the depth, but don't be overly concerned with minor bumps and depressions. If you find that you have excavated too much at some point, fill in that area and tamp firmly. Soft spots could cause the paving to settle unevenly.

Build forms for the planter foundation with 2 × 4s. Don't be tempted to use the redwood framing because the redwood would probably be stained by the concrete. At 4-foot intervals, stake the forms into place with 1 × 2s driven securely into the ground. To make removal of the forms easier after the foundation has set, coat the inside of the boards with crankcase oil. After the forms are in place, check each side and the corners to make sure they are level. Using a garden hose, thoroughly soak the excavation within the form. Wait until the surface water disappears before pouring the concrete. When concrete is poured on dry soil, moisture is drawn out too rapidly. This can cause an improper cure that could result in a weak foundation.

Place 1 part cement, 2½ parts sand, and 3 parts gravel into a wheelbarrow and mix with a shovel. Blend the contents thoroughly. Form a hollow in the center of the mixture and add a small amount of water. Use a garden hoe or a shovel to thoroughly mix the contents. Repeat this procedure using approximately 3 quarts of water for each shovelful of cement. Too much water will weaken the concrete and too little water will make portions of mix too dry to set up properly.

Shovel the concrete mix into the forms until the concrete is level with the top of the forms. Tamp the surface until level and fill in any low spots. The concrete should set for at least one hour. During this time, hose off the wheelbarrow and other tools. As the concrete hardens, use a stiff bristled broom to roughen the surface. This will create a bonding surface for the bricks.

To obtain proper curing, wet the concrete and cover it with burlap or straw in order to retard evaporation. In warm weather, keep the foundation damp for at least three days. In cooler weather, keep the foundation damp for as much as a week. After three or four days, you can begin laying brick. However, the forms should remain in place for at least one week.

THE PLANTER

The height of the planter is 13¾ inches, and 5 courses of brick are used. Double rows of running bond are used for the first four courses. Each brick is offset half the length of the one next to it and the one below it. The top course is laid sideways across the course beneath it. This ties the rows together (Fig. 3-5).

Before you permanently set the bricks in place, position a few courses without mortar in order to check the accuracy of the measurements. Remember to allow for approximately ½ inch between each course for

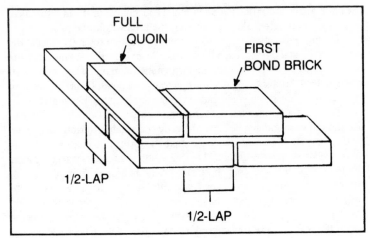

Fig. 5-5. Corner construction for one-half bond.

mortar joints. It should not be necessary to cut any bricks for the planter. If everything fits properly, spray the brick pile with water about one hour before you begin laying brick. The bricks should be damp but not dripping wet. Too much water will dilute the mortar and cause it to slip off the bricks when placed.

To form mortar, mix 1 part portland cement, ½ part hydrated lime and 4½ parts sand. Do not mix more than you can use in half an hour. Mortar should have the consistency of soft mud that slides easily from the shovel. If the mortar becomes too stiff, add a small quantity of water and mix thoroughly. Dampen the foundation lightly before you begin to lay the bricks.

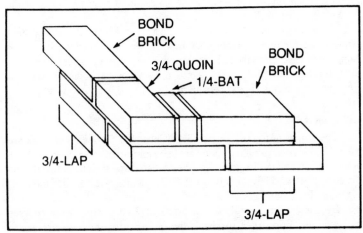

Fig. 5-6. Corner construction for three-quarter bond.

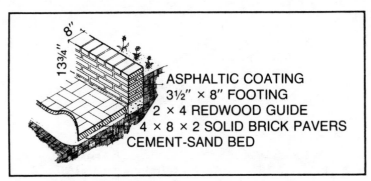

ASPHALTIC COATING
3½" × 8" FOOTING
2 × 4 REDWOOD GUIDE
4 × 8 × 2 SOLID BRICK PAVERS
CEMENT-SAND BED

Fig. 5-7. The top course of the planter is laid lengthwise.

The finished wall will have a thickness of 2 courses of brick—plus a ½-inch mortar joint. This is equal to the length of one brick.

Build the corners (Figs. 3-5 and 3-6) first by laying the two courses four rows high and dovetailed at right angles. Starting with the inside course, use a trowel to lay ½ inch of mortar on the foundation, about the length of two bricks. As you gain experience, you will be able to lay three or more bricks at a time. Furrow the mortar bed with the trowel point. Butter the end of a brick and set it in place. Clip off excess mortar and return it to the mortar board. Butter the end of another brick and position it against the first. Complete the inside course and then build the outside row, buttering the edges and sides to bond the two courses.

Use a straightedge and level to plumb the corners. After you finish all four corners, push nails into the soft mortar of the second course at each corner. Run a length of string between corners to serve as a guide while you lay the remainder of the bricks. Use a level and straightedge frequently to keep the walls plumb.

After the first four courses are completed, set the top course in place. Techniques for laying mortar and positioning bricks are the same except that the top course is laid lengthwise (Fig. 5-7).

Tool the joints with a pointing trowel or a section of ¾-inch inch steel pipe to produce smooth, concave surfaces. During hot weather, wet the brickwork occasionally the first few weeks after construction to allow the mortar to cure slowly. If mortar stains remain on the brick, muriatic (hydrochloric) acid diluted with 9 parts water can be used to remove the stains. For this job, wear rubber gloves, and protection for your eyes. First, soak the brickwork with water and then scrub on the solution with a stiff, bristled brush. Rinse the scrubbed area at once with water. After the mortar has cured, waterproof the inside of the planter with an asphalt coating.

THE PATIO FOUNDATION

The first step in building the patio foundation is to assemble the frame

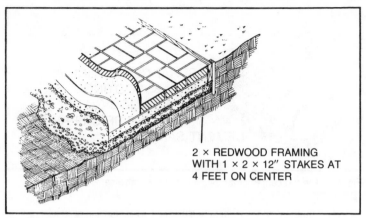

2 × REDWOOD FRAMING
WITH 1 × 2 × 12" STAKES AT
4 FEET ON CENTER

Fig. 5-8. Mortared paving and redwood edging.

of redwood 2 × 4s. The inside dimensions should be 6' ½" × 14' × 1". Check the measurements before you drive two 8d galvanized nails into each corner of the frame (Fig. 5-4).

Position the frame in the excavation. At approximately 4-foot intervals, drive 1-×-2 redwood stakes into the ground outside the frame. The corners of the frame should be square. Check the top edges of the frame against the marks on the grading stakes that were used to guide the excavation. The top of the frame and the top of the stakes should be even with the top of the finished paving. Nail the frame to the stakes (see Fig. 5-8).

Shovel sand into the center of the patio excavation. Leave a few shovelfuls of sand for later use in filling joints. Add one sack of cement at a time and thoroughly mix it with the sand. If the sand is at all damp, the mixture will begin to set. Therefore, you should spread the mixture with the rake as quickly as possible to a depth of about 1¾ inches.

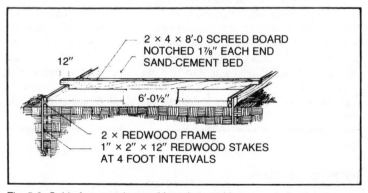

2 × 4 × 8'-0 SCREED BOARD
NOTCHED 1⅞" EACH END
SAND-CEMENT BED

12"

6'-0½"

2 × REDWOOD FRAME
1" × 2" × 12" REDWOOD STAKES
AT 4 FOOT INTERVALS

Fig. 5-9. Guide frame and screed board assembly.

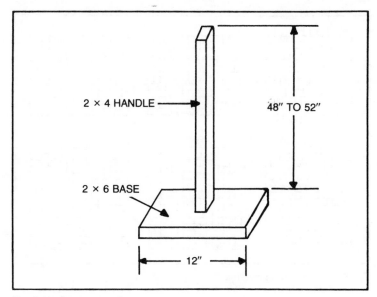

2 × 4 HANDLE

48" TO 52"

2 × 6 BASE

12"

Fig. 5-10. A tamper tool.

Use an 8-foot long, 2-×-4 straightedge to screed the surface. The straightedge can be notched with the ends resting on the redwood frame (Fig. 5-9). Cut the notches 1 foot from the ends and 1⅞ inches deep. Draw the straightedge across the frame to level the patio bed. Fill in the low spots and repeat the screeding procedure until the bed is level.

Tamp the patio bed so that it is firm. A tamper can be built by nailing a short section of 2 × 6 to a 2-×-4 handle (Fig. 5-10). Fill in any low spots and repeat the screeding procedure.

LAYING THE MORTARLESS PAVING

Once the patio bed is prepared, begin laying bricks from the frame edge inward. Start at one corner and position the bricks tightly against the others in the pattern you prefer (Figs. 5-7 and 5-11). Stand on the laid bricks as you work rather than on the sand/cement surface. Use a mallet to firmly tap each brick into place. If the base has been properly prepared, the bricks should be level and each course should fit easily into the redwood frame.

After the last brick has been placed, fill the joints with sand. Use a broom to sweep the surface clean. Wet the joints with a fine spray of water to compact the sand. Be very careful not to wash out the sand. All joints should be flush with the bricks. It might be necessary to refill some joints with sand and spray again. The patio is now ready for use.

BUILDING A PATIO ON CONCRETE

In a climate where winters are severe, the patio should be built on a

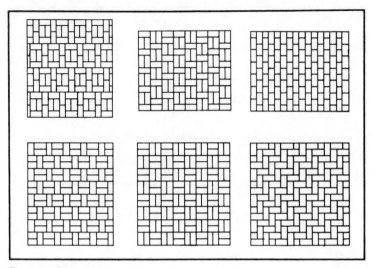

Fig. 5-11. Brick paving patterns.

concrete slab, and the brick paving should be set in mortar. Because mortar joints are used, building brick rather than paving brick is used for the patio.

The planter is constructed as previously detailed, except that the foundation is dug deeper. Check local building codes to determine the frost line for your area. The overall dimensions of the planter are the same. The excavation of the patio, however, increases to 6' 7" × 15' ½" to allow for ½-inch mortar joints and the guide frame. Lay out the section with stakes as previously described and excavate to a depth of about 9¾ inches.

The concrete slab is 6' 4½ × 14' 10½". Build forms from plywood or

Table 5-1. Concrete in Cubic Feet.

	Footings and 3" slab				Sand Bed	
Col. 1 Footing Length (feet)	Col. 2 3½" × 8" Footing (cu. ft.)	Col. 3 8" × 12" Footing (cu. ft.)	Col. 4 Patio Area (sq. ft.)	Col. 5 3" concrete slab (cu. ft.)	Col. 6 1" Bed (cu. ft.)	Col. 7 2" Bed (cu. ft.)
1	.19	.67	10	2.5	.83	1.66
2	.39	1.33	20	5.0	1.66	3.32
3	.58	2.00	30	7.5	2.49	4.98
4	.78	2.66	40	10.0	3.32	6.64
5	.97	3.33	50	12.5	4.15	8.30
6	1.16	4.00	60	15.0	4.98	9.96
7	1.36	4.66	70	17.5	5.81	11.62
8	1.55	5.33	80	20.0	6.64	13.28
9	1.75	6.00	90	22.5	7.47	14.94
10	1.94	6.66	100	25.0	8.30	16.60
40.5	7.86	27.00	108	27.0	8.96	17.93
139.2	27.00	92.69	150	37.5	12.45	24.90

2-inch lumber and position the forms in the excavation. The top of the poured concrete slab should be 2¾ inches below the top of the finished brick paving. Support the forms with stakes driven into the ground at 4-foot intervals. Refer to previously described planter foundation details.

Lay a 4-inch-deep gravel base inside the foundation forms. Consult Table 5-1 to estimate the amount of concrete you will need. A 3-inch slab of concrete for each section requires approximately 1 cubic yard of concrete. Probably the most convenient method is to order ready-mixed concrete delivered by truck. Don't order more than 3 cubic yards at one time, and be sure to have someone at the site to help you.

If you want to mix the concrete yourself, rent a mixing machine. Mixing by hand is very strenuous and time-consuming labor. Refer to Tables 5-2 and 5-3 for the quantities of cement, sand, gravel, brick, and mortar needed to construct the patio and planter.

The amount of cement you can mix at one time depends on the size of the machine you rent. Put 1 part cement and 2½ parts sand in the machine and mix thoroughly. Next, mix in 3 parts gravel. Add water and tumble for

Table 5-2. Material List.

Patio Material		Number of 6' × 14' Patio Sections			
		1	2	3	4
Brick Pavers, 4″ × 8″ × 2″ (includes 5% waste)	=	400	800	1200	1600
Portland Cement (94 lb. sacks)	=	4	8	12	16
Sand, damp & loose (pounds)	=	1090	2180	3270	4360
Redwood framing, 2″ × 4″ × 8 ft.1	=	6	12	18	24
Redwood stakes, 1″ × 2″ × 12″	=	10	18	26	34
Nails, 2 pounds of 8d galvanized common					

Planter Wall Material		Footings		Mortar		Total
Face Brick, 3¾″ × 2¼″ × 8″: 440 units (includes 5% waste)						
Portland Cement (94 lb. sacks)	=	1⅜	+	1¾	=	3⅛
Sand, damp & loose (pounds)	=	287	+	696	=	983
Hydrated Lime (50 lb. sacks)	=	—	+	¾	=	¾
Old lumber for temporary footing forms						

Mortared Paving on Concrete Slab		Number of 6' × 14' Patio Sections			
		1	2	3	4
Standard Brick, 3¾″ × 2¼″ × 8″ (includes 5% waste)	=	400	800	1200	1600
Portland Cement (94 lb. sacks)	=	3	6	9	12
Hydrated Lime (50 lb. sacks)	=	⅔	1⅓	2	2⅔
Sand, damp & loose (pounds)	=	772	1544	2316	3088
Redwood framming, 2″ × 6″ × 8 ft.1	=	6	12	18	24
Redwood stakes, 1″ × 2″ × 12″	=	10	20	30	40
3″ Concrete Slab: Portland Cement (sacks)	=	6	12	18	24
Sand (pounds)	=	1213	2426	3639	4852
Base gravel (pounds) Gravel (pounds)	=	1765	3530	5295	7060
	=	3640	7280	10,920	14,560

(1) Other lengths, such as 10, 12 and 14 ft. can be used.

Table 5-3. A Brick Quantity and Cubic Feet of Mortar.

	Patio Brick and Mortar				Wall Brick and Mortar			
	Brick Units		Mortar (cu. ft.)		Brick Units		Mortar (cu. ft.)	
Col. 1	Col. 2	Col. 3	Col. 4	Col. 5	Col. 6	Col. 7	Col. 8	Col. 9
Area of Patio or Wall (sq. ft.)	4" × 8" solid pavers	3¾" × 8" solid standards	½" joints with 3¾ × 8 units	½" mortar leveling bed	8" walls	4" walls	8" walls	4" walls
1	4.5	4.0	.033	.042	12.32	6.16	.186	.072
2	9.0	8.0	.066	.083	24.64	12.32	.371	.144
3	13.5	12.0	.099	.125	36.96	18.48	.557	.216
4	18.0	16.0	.132	.167	49.28	24.64	.743	.288
5	22.5	20.0	.165	.209	61.60	30.80	.929	.360
10	45.0	40.0	.330	.417	123.20	61.60	1.857	.720
25	112.5	100.0	.825	1.043	308.00	154.00	4.643	1.800
50	225.0	200.0	1.650	2.085	616.00	308.00	9.285	3.600
75	337.5	300.0	2.475	3.128	924.00	462.00	13.928	5.400
100	450.00	400.0	3.300	4.170	1232.00	616.00	18.570	7.200

about 3 minutes. Pour the concrete into a wheelbarrow and then into the excavation.

Spread the concrete throughout the foundation and use a straightedge (Fig. 5-12) to obtain a smooth level surface that is even with the top of the forms. Use a wooden float (Figs. 5-13 and 5-14) to work out any irregular spots, but don't overwork the concrete. Overworking could result in a less durable foundation.

After the concrete sets for an hour, use a stiff-bristled broom to roughen the surface. This will provide a bonding surface for the brick

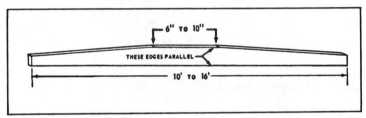

Fig. 5-12. A mason's straightedge.

Fig. 5-13. A long handle wood float.

Fig. 5-14. A wooden float.

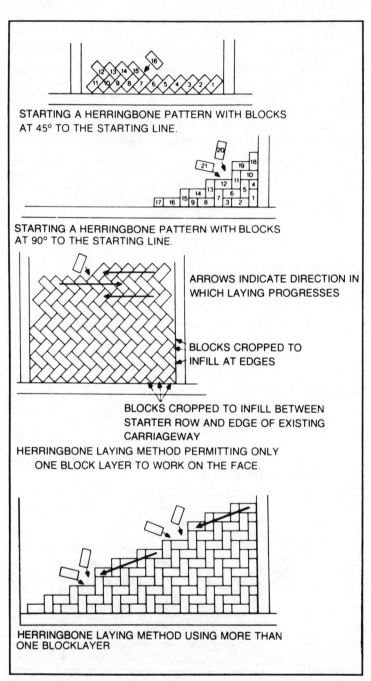

STARTING A HERRINGBONE PATTERN WITH BLOCKS AT 45° TO THE STARTING LINE.

STARTING A HERRINGBONE PATTERN WITH BLOCKS AT 90° TO THE STARTING LINE.

ARROWS INDICATE DIRECTION IN WHICH LAYING PROGRESSES

BLOCKS CROPPED TO INFILL AT EDGES

BLOCKS CROPPED TO INFILL BETWEEN STARTER ROW AND EDGE OF EXISTING CARRIAGEWAY

HERRINGBONE LAYING METHOD PERMITTING ONLY ONE BLOCK LAYER TO WORK ON THE FACE.

HERRINGBONE LAYING METHOD USING MORE THAN ONE BLOCKLAYER

Fig. 5-15. Typical brick paving installation procedures.

mortar. Water the concrete and cover it with burlap or straw to obtain proper curing. Keep the concrete damp for at least a week before you lay the brick.

Remove the forms and position the 2 × 4 redwood frame. Remember that the frame should extend 2¾ inches above the slab. Drive redwood stakes into the ground at approximately 4-foot intervals and nail the frame to the stakes.

The techniques for laying mortared paving (Fig. 5-15) are quite similar to the methods used for building the planter. Mix 1 part portland cement, ¼ part hydrated lime and 3 parts sand for mortar. Begin paving one corner by laying a ½-inch bed of mortar that is large enough for two bricks. Butter the brick sides and edges and position them according to the pattern you prefer. Continue the pattern with ½-inch mortar joint between each brick.

Joints can be tooled or they can be left flush with the bricks. Use a damp cloth to wipe excess mortar from the bricks as you work. After completion, keep the patio damp for several days to obtain proper curing.

Tools

Shovel
Wheelbarrow
Garden hose
Garden rake
Framing square
2-foot hand level
Mason's string
Mason's line level
Hammer
Bricklayer's trowel
Wooden float (long handle)
Hand wooden float
Mason's pointing tool (or short section of ¾-inch steel pipe)
Broom (stiff bristled)
Broad-bladed brick chisel
Tamper
Screed board
2- ×-4 straightedge
Burlap or straw
Powered mortar mixer (optional)

Materials

To estimate the amount of material needed to construct the patio and planter, refer to Tables 5-1, 5-2 and 5-3. If the climate in your area includes freeze/thaw cycles, use SW grade brick. Severe weather brick is capable of resisting harsh climatic changes.

Be sure to plan each step ahead of time. Study each diagram and all the instructions for this project before you actually begin construction.

Project 6

Skylight Installation and Care

There are many types of prefabricated skylights on the market. Shapes include round, oval, square, rectangular, triangle and ridge, flat, domed, hipped and barrel. The transparent surface can be plastic glazed, clear, translucent, gray, or bronze. Skylight frames are made of wood, plastic, or metal. Custom-designed skylights also are available.

Self-flashing skylights (Fig. 6-1) are used on roofs with less than a 3 in 12 pitch and have a built-in curb and flange for flashing. The *curb-mounted skylight* (Fig. 6-2) is designed for roofs with a slope greater than 3 in 12, and it needs a curb and flashing built as the unit is installed.

INSTALLING SKYLIGHTS

The tools (Fig. 6-3) you will need for installing your skylight include a measuring tape, a carpenter's square, a hammer, framing nails, roofing nails, a keyhole saw, roofing mastic, a handsaw or power saw, tin snips, header lumber, framing lumber, and finish materials. If you're installing a curb-mounted skylight, you'll also need a screwdriver, pan head wood screws (rust resistant), aluminum flashing (curb height plus 6 inches) and 2-×-8 or larger dimension lumber.

Determine if your rafters are spaced 16 or 24 inches apart, on centers. Rafter thickness sometimes varies depending on the age of the home. Therefore spacing between your roof rafters might vary from Fig. 6-4. The frame and opening in the roof should be sized according to the inside dimensions of the skylight.

The first installation step for self-flashing and curb-mounted skylights is to locate the position for the skylight (Figs. 6-5, 6-6, and 6-7). For an open-beam ceiling, drive a long nail from the inside of the house up through

76

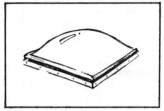

Fig. 6-1. A self-flashing skylight.

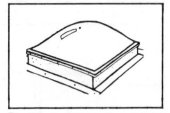

Fig. 6-2. A curb-mounted skylight.

the roof at each corner of the planned skylight opening. Follow this same procedure for a conventional house except it must be done from the attic or crawl space.

On the roof surface, locate the nails driven through the roof. Remove the roofing material in the area bound by the four nails. *After* supporting existing rafters that require cutting, cut a hole through the roof surface. Except for the bottom of the opening, carefully lay back shingles and felt paper an additional 6 inches around the perimeter of the opening. Be careful not to cut through nails or staples when cutting the hole through the roof.

The third step is to install headers following the rafter framing plans. Rafter supports can now be removed.

Self-Flashing Skylight

If you are installing a self-flashing skylight on a sloping roof, the fourth step is to make sure the shingles are even with or a row beyond the bottom edge of the opening. Place two 1-inch wide by ⅛-inch thick beads of roofing mastic 1 inch apart around the perimeter of the opening. Stay about an inch away from the edge (Fig. 6-8).

With skylight weep holes (arrows in Fig. 6-9), toward the bottom of

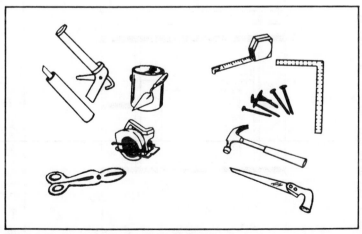

Fig. 6-3. Tools needed to install a skylight.

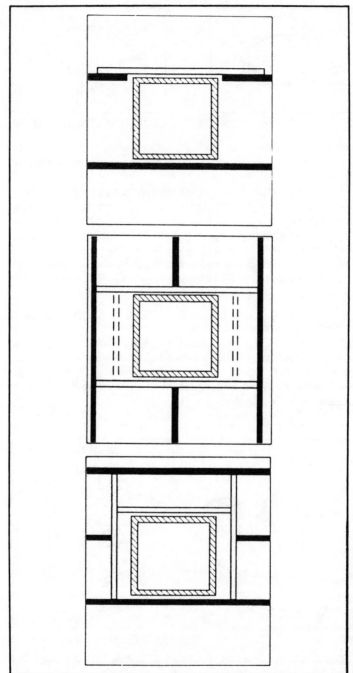

Fig. 6-4. Framing the skylight.

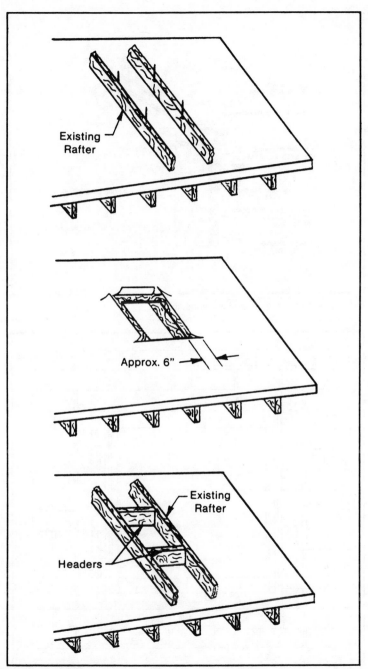

Fig. 6-5. Installing the skylight well.

Existing Rafter

Approx. 6"

Existing Rafter

Headers

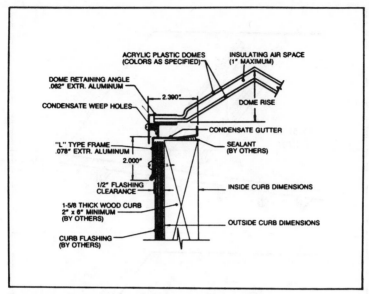

Fig. 6-6. A cross section of skylight installation.

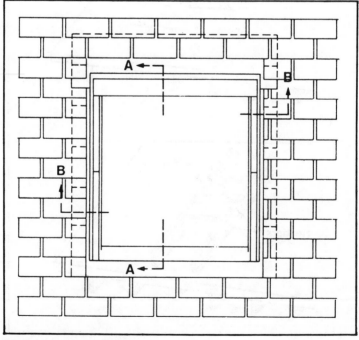

Fig. 6-7. The skylight opening.

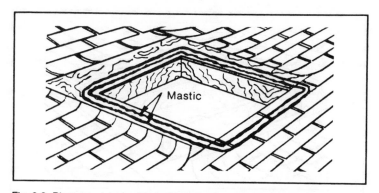

Fig. 6-8. Place two 1-inch wide by ⅛-inch thick beads of roofing mastic 1 inch apart around the perimeter of the opening.

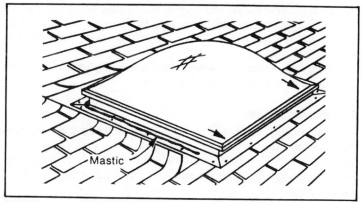

Fig. 6-9. Center the skylight in the opening and secure it to the roof with roofing nails.

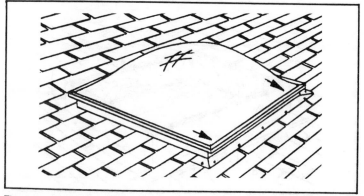

Fig. 6-10. Replace shingles and seal.

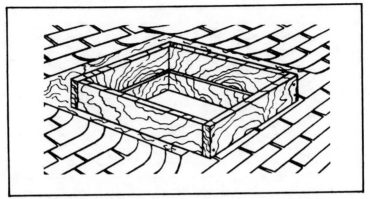

Fig. 6-11. Build the wood curb directly over the rafter frame opening.

the opening, center the skylight over the opening and secure it to the roof with roofing nails through punched holes in the flanges *only*. Place another bead of roofing mastic on top of the skylight flanges at the top and bottom sides.

Then replace shingles. Do not nail through the skylight flange. Mastic is adequate to seal the shingles (Fig. 6-10).

Curb-Mounted Skylight

The installation procedures for curb-mounted skylights are similar to the procedures for installing self-flashing skylights. First, apply roofing mastic ⅛ inch thick, as wide as the curb lumber, around the entire perimeter of the opening. Construct the wood curb directly over the rafter frame opening (Fig. 6-11).

Now fit aluminum sheet-metal flashing to the outside of the curb (Fig. 6-12). Flashing must go to the top of the curb with a 3-inch flange around the

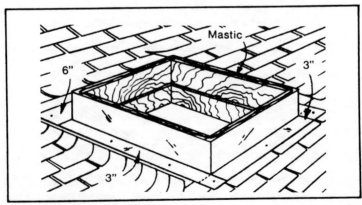

Fig. 6-12. Install metal flashing.

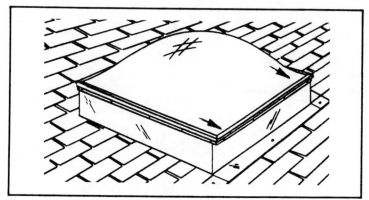
Fig. 6-13. Install shingles and secure the skylight.

base except for a 6-inch flange on the top side. Seal the undersides and the top of the metal flanges with roofing mastic.

Install shingles and apply an ⅛-inch bead of roofing mastic around the entire perimeter on the top of the curb. With skylight weep holes (arrows in Fig. 6-13) toward the bottom of the opening, place the skylight on the curb and secure it with rust-resistant, pan-head wood screws through punched holes in the frame. Don't overtighten the screws.

The Skylight Well

Homes with conventional rather than cathedral ceilings must also have a skylight well to allow the light captured by the roof skylight to enter rooms below the ceiling. Figure 6-14 illustrates three common types of skylight wells: the straight well, the angled well, and the expanded well. A well that is expanded will admit more light and disperse it better to illuminate the whole room. The appropriate design for your installation, however, depends on your needs and the relationships between the sun, the skylight, and room below.

To install the skylight well, first take measurements to locate the planned location of the skylight. Use walls and stairways as reference points.

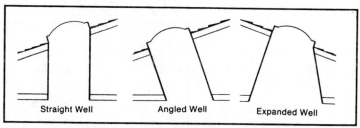
Straight Well   Angled Well   Expanded Well

Fig. 6-14. Three common types of skylight wells.

Fig. 6-15. Lay out the ceiling opening on the attic floor.

Go to the crawl space or attic and check your measurements. The ceiling opening might have to be shifted to one side so it will be aligned correctly with ceiling joists. Lay out the ceiling opening on the attic floor (Fig. 6-15).

Using a plumb bob, lay out the roof opening (depending on the style of light well) above the ceiling opening. Now cut the hole in the ceiling as shown in Fig. 6-16. Brace across the ceiling joists as required. Install headers between the ceiling joists.

Finish the framing of the skylight well. See Figs. 6-17 through 6-22. The example shown in Fig. 6-17 is for a light well that is expanded to allow more light into the room. The well can be lined with the finishing materials of your choice. Be sure to insulate around the light well. If painting is required to finish off the light well, mask off the entire skylight to prevent paint splatters.

INSTALLING ROOF WINDOWS

A roof window is a rotary window installed in the roof that opens to allow ventilation (Fig. 6-20). Installing a roof window is similar to installing

Fig. 6-16. Cut the hole in the ceiling.

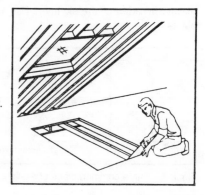

Fig. 6-17. Finish framing the skylight well.

skylights, but there are enough differences to require separate installation instructions.

For comfortable operation by hand, the height from the finished floor level to the top of the window should be 6 foot 3 inches to 6 foot 9 inches. As recommended, a horizontal soffit at the head (A of Fig. 6-20) and a vertical lining at the sill (B of Fig. 6-20) will give more headroom, better light distribution, and an attractive appearance. If possible, arrange the vertical lining (B of Fig. 6-20) as shown with the heat source below to ensure free flow of air over the glass (C of Fig. 6-20) minimizing condensation when the window is closed. Manual and power remote controls are available for out-of-reach windows.

Figure 6-4 illustrates three ways that rafters can be modified to accommodate roof windows.

Before installation, the typical roof window must be disassembled. Separate the sash from the frame and remove the exterior cladding pieces from the frame (Fig. 6-21).

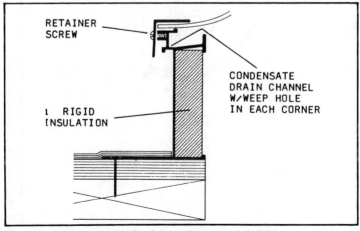

Fig. 6-18. Construction details of the curb-mounted skylight.

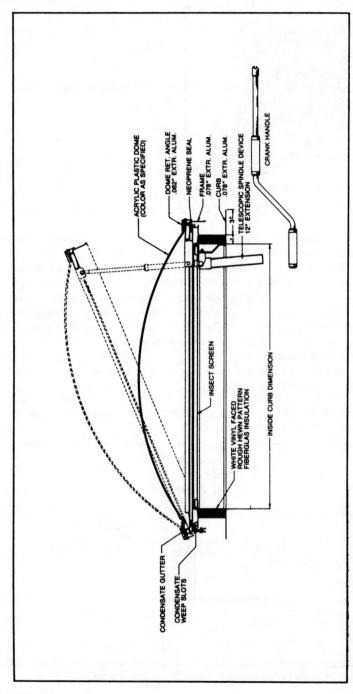

ACRYLIC PLASTIC DOME
(COLOR AS SPECIFIED)

DOME RET. ANGLE
.062" EXTR. ALUM.

NEOPRENE SEAL

FRAME
.078" EXTR. ALUM.

CURB
.078" EXTR. ALUM.

TELESCOPIC SPINDLE DEVICE
12" EXTENSION

CRANK HANDLE

INSECT SCREEN

WHITE VINYL FACED
ROUGH HEWN PATTERN
FIBERGLAS INSULATION

INSIDE CURB DIMENSION

CONDENSATE GUTTER

CONDENSATE
WEEP SLOTS

Fig. 6-19. Details of a venting skylight.

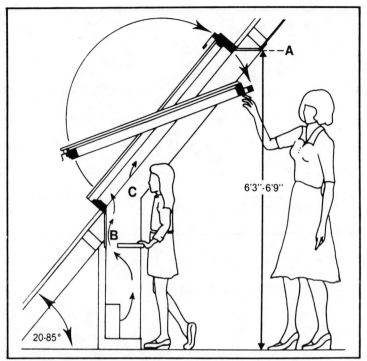

Fig. 6-20. Using the roof window.

Install the frame in the roof. Screw the mounting brackets into the sheathing. Level the sill and take diagonal measures to obtain squareness.

Install the sill flashing section (Fig. 6-22). It should be even with the front edge of the shingles. Nail the side pieces to the frame. See Figs. 6-23 and 6-24.

Install the step flashing pieces. They should be interwoven with each

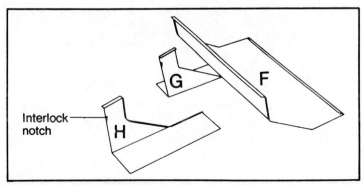

Fig. 6-21. Roof window flashing.

87

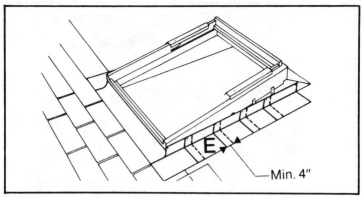

Fig. 6-22. Install the sill flashing section.

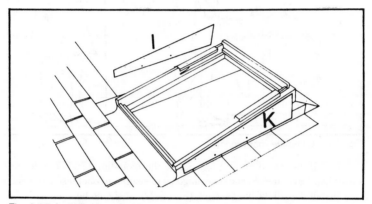

Fig. 6-23. Install side units.

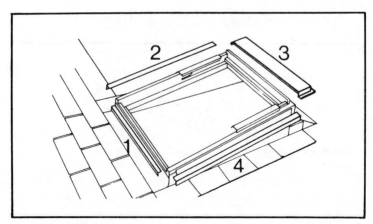

Fig. 6-24. Install casings.

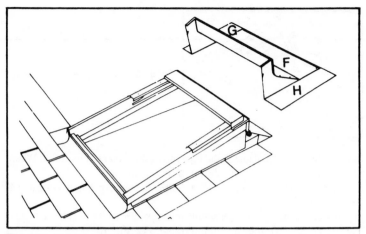

Fig. 6-25. Install top step flashing pieces.

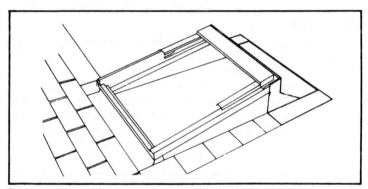

Fig. 6-26. Framing and flashing are installed.

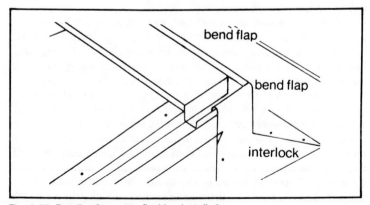

Fig. 6-27. Details of top step flashing installation.

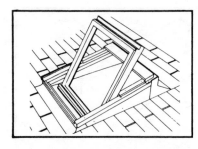

Fig. 6-28. The installed roof window.

layer of shingles. Then install the top step flashing piece (Fig. 6-25). When necessary, cut the pieces as shown in the illustrations.

Replace exterior claddings (Fig. 6-26). Remember that pieces 2 and 4 are not interchangeable.

Install the head flashing section and interlock with the side claddings (Fig. 6-27). Replace the sash in the frame. See Fig. 6-28.

Wood finishes should be re-treated soon after installation.

SKYLIGHT CARE

To clean glass skylights and roof windows, use common household window cleaner. To clean acrylic domes and to remove electrostatic charges, wash with nonabrasive soap or detergent and water. Use your bare hand (no rags) to feel and dislodge any dirt that has hardened on the skylight dome. A soft, clean cloth or sponge should be used only to carry water to the dome. After the dome has been thoroughly rinsed with clean water, dry the dome with a clean, damp chamois or cotton flannel. Rough or hard cloths should not be used because they will scratch a plastic dome.

Where water cannot be used freely, such as interior installations, the dome should first be dusted lightly—but not wiped—with a clean, soft cloth. The dome is then wiped carefully with a soft, wet chamois or cloth. The chamois or cloth should be rinsed off in clean water to keep it free from dirt that can scratch the finish.

To remove grease, oil, or roof caulking compounds, use kerosene or pure aliphatic naptha with no aromatic content. Solvents such as benzene, acetone, fire-extinguisher fluid, carbon tetrachloride, dry cleaning fluid, lacquer thinners, and gasoline should *not* be used because they will attack the dome's acrylic surface. Scouring compounds should not be used.

If there is no great amount of scratching visible after cleaning the dome, it should be waxed with a high-quality paste or liquid wax that does not contain compounds that could scratch the dome. Waxing will improve the appearance of the dome by filling in minor scratches. Apply the wax in a thin, even coat and bring it to a high gloss by rubbing lightly with a dry, soft cloth such as cotton flannel. Avoid excessive rubbing with a dry cloth because it will cause scratches as well as build up an electrostatic charge that will attract dust particles to the dome's surface. Blotting the dome with a clean, damp cloth or chamois will remove the charge as well as any dust.

Index